MAKING SENSE OF GRAMMAR

John Clark Jordan
Former Dean of the Graduate School
University of Arkansas

Edited and with an Introduction by

J. R. LeMaster
Baylor University

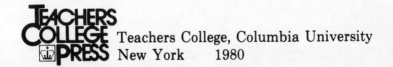 Teachers College, Columbia University
New York   1980

Published by Teachers College Press
1234 Amsterdam Avenue, New York, NY 10027

Library of Congress Cataloging in Publication Data
Jordan, John Clark, 1883-
   Making sense of grammar.
   Revision of the 1962 ed. published under title:
Grammar for the common reader.
   Includes index.
   1. English language—Grammar—1950- I. LeMaster,
J. R., 1934- II. Title.
PE1105.J6   1980   425   79-24986
ISBN 0-8077-2577-3
Designed by Julie E. Scott
8   7   6   5   4   3   2   1
87 86 85 84 83 82 81 80
Manufactured in the U.S.A.

From whence he came in search of a tongue he returned,
and cherishing what he had found among the ruins
he left us here to carry on the task that he'd begun.

                                        J. R. LeMaster

Contents

	Introduction	vii
1.	A Point of View	1
2.	An Incident and Its Implications	4
3.	What a Sentence Is	7
4.	Simple Sentence Patterns	14
5.	Simple Modifiers	29
6.	Prepositional Phrases	38
7.	Inflection	43
8.	Certain Matters of Importance	55
9.	Compound Sentences	67
10.	Complex Sentences	72
11.	Verbals	85
12.	Punctuation	106
	Index	115

Introduction

In the decade of the fifties, when I was an undergraduate at Defiance College, I had the good fortune of studying my own language under one of those men who are gifted with unusual insight. Long after such a man is dead one carries around something of his genius in an effort to preserve it. There are two or three reasons why this might happen, but none of them seem to be very conclusive. In one sense, at least, the entire matter can be written off as an overdose of hero worship. Heroes, however, command respect that in former times would have been paid to the gods, for it is that which is godlike—that which elevates the individual man above the mass of humanity —that both inspires and mystifies. In our American culture, we are indeed hard put to explain the demise of the intellectual hero in our time.

Heroes, intellectual and otherwise, immortalize themselves by positing indestructible images of themselves in the heads of those who would believe. On the other hand, those who believe in and follow the hero—especially the intellectual hero—are the ones who stand to gain, for they are always being placed in positions that require testing the genius of the one who came before. The result is an insatiable appetite for knowledge—an appetite that serves both the hero and the worshippers through a perennial test by fire.

Thus it has been in my twenty-year courtship with my memory of having been a student of John Clark Jordan, even as it was with his memory of having been a student of Otto Jespersen at Columbia University. When Dr. Jordan retired from the University of Arkansas and came to Defiance College in the fifties, he brought with him what seemed to me more common sense about language and language study than I had ever heard before, and certainly more than I have heard since. He was a man in love with his native tongue, always talking about it as though he had just discovered it.

In 1949 Rinehart and Company published a strange little book by Dr. Jordan entitled *A Grammar for Heretics*. The title alone is curious, as though its author did not expect it to be well received. The book was ahead of its time, as the title indicates. Nonetheless, knowing that his book was an anachronism, Dr. Jordan revised it and prepared it for a second publication with the title *Grammar for the Common Reader*, which was finally published by Pageant Press in 1962. The change in titles indicates that he thought the time was right, but again he was to be disappointed. Throughout the fifties linguistic science as such had come into its own, and as a result, for the most part, language study became increasingly esoteric. In the sixties, stormy as they were, public schools, colleges, and universities kept pace with the times by reacting negatively to anything that might be considered traditional; and in many cases language study was abandoned as unnecessary and cruel punishment inflicted upon others by those belonging to "the establishment." Nonverbal communication was in vogue. The dilemma, therefore, was that language study was eliminated almost altogether for the traditional was too stifling and what was new was either inaccessible or incomprehensible.

When *Newsweek* published "Why Johnny Can't Write" on December 8, 1975, no one who had been grappling with freshman theme papers was surprised to learn that Johnny actually can't write. Educators had known all along that he can't speak either. What was surprising—and continues to be—is that it took so long, even to the point of a pending national

crisis, for them to accept the fact that language study is necessary. Now that they have recognized that they have a problem,
how long will it take to accept the fact that language study must
make sense? A return to basics, if by that is meant a return to
the so-called "rules of grammar," does not make sense and will
not solve the dilemma. Neither will a highly esoteric approach
to language study in the name of linguistics—especially if
linguistic texts continue to ignore the level of national intelligence or aptitude for learning. What is needed for our time
is a common sense approach, one that accounts for the way the
language functions. Such an approach must begin with the form
classes and proceed to an examination of their functions and
relations—always defining, explaining, and illustrating. The
difference is that of "learning" language as opposed to "learning about" language. As in learning anything, to learn language
is to internalize it in such a way that it makes a difference in the
way we function, in such a way that it becomes important because it makes sense in light of what we already know.

What impressed me about Dr. Jordan's grammar in the fifties was that it avoided extremes. Rather it (and he) dwelled on
the idea of understanding. Perhaps the best I can do at this
point is to quote directly from the preface to the 1962 edition:

> This book is intended to give a brief insight into the way the
> English language works. It is based on the conviction that,
> though a person will never learn what grammar is by memorizing
> definitions, he may eventually get to know the feel of gram-
> matical relationships through contact with many sentences in
> their various forms and structures, and through being brought to
> a kind of awareness of the circumstances out of which sentences
> arise. I have assumed that the mind of the reader will respond to
> the material presented to it; and that through the pleasure of
> learning, it will acquire some knowledge of the way sentences are
> made and of the principles upon which they rest.

What impresses me about the grammar now is that it still does
for me what it did in the fifties. It makes my language sound
just as important to me now as it did then. It never takes the
language from me under the pretense of turning it back in some

purified or stilted form, but rather it allows me to hold my language within and view it there, as though it were the Kingdom of God binding together all who speak and write it. The intent expressed in the concluding paragraph of the preface to the 1962 edition is carried out through the entire text:

> I have ever had in mind the resourcefulness, versatility, and beauty of our language; and I have tried to keep my remarks as free as possible from the pedantry which has frequently hindered our effective and spontaneous use of this instrument to which we owe so much devotion and study and loyalty. I have tried to understand it as it was and is. Vital it has always been, living now as through the centuries, equal to the demands put upon it, whether by poet, scientist, philosopher, or simple workman carrying on the affairs of his humble existence.

In doing my job as editor I have made no major changes in the text of Dr. Jordan's grammar. His genius shines through on every page, and I prefer to leave it that way. On the other hand, I have on occasion changed the wording of a brief passage, mostly within a sentence, to make the passage a little clearer or more cogent for our times. I have also removed some punctuation marks that appear to me to be superfluous, but I have always kept the meaning of the text as Dr. Jordan wrote it. To change that, I fear, would be to render the text invalid, at which point I could no longer believe in either the text or its author.

J. R. LeMaster
Professor of English
Baylor University

1   A Point of View

Agreat deal of stodgy nonsense, it must be admitted, has been said and written about grammar. Part of it has come from ignorance of what lies back of the way we say things here in America. Part of it has come from making grammar consist of definitions and elaborate classifications that can be learned only as acts of memory. Part of it, the most damaging part, has come from the mistaken notion that grammar is a mass of rules about what is and what is not correct. The result is that many a youngster with red blood in his veins and ideas in his head either bogs down in despair or quits in disgust. He is through with English forever—all of which is greatly to be deplored.

A friend of mine said to me one day when we were talking on this subject that he thought he was very fortunate to have been born speaking the English language, for, said he, "I'm sure I never could have learned it." As a matter of fact, this was a right clever fellow; his remark shows that. But what he said is just my point. Why should an intelligent American living in a typical American neighborhood, trained in a typical American school, have grown to manhood with a feeling that his native language was difficult or even impossible to learn?

Suppose you were to try quoting my friend's remark to one of the backwoodsmen of the Ozark hills. He would not understand what you were talking about. He would not be conscious himself of any difficulty in saying what he wanted to say.

> I'm not a cow man myself. I'm a goat man. They's more money in 'em and me and goats just naturally git along. They come in at night. A goat likes home; and they stay together. You can drive twenty goats like they was one. And when one kicks—which ain't often—they don't mash the bucket flat.*

He would not worry about errors in diction and syntax and end up saying nothing. He would speak the true, unconscious speech of the soil.

The speech ways of the folk are the foundation of language. Correct English is at best only a refinement, (very limited and very much on the surface) of the folk speech. The common people have developed for themselves the great resources of our language. They have evolved the word order of the English sentence; they have developed our prepositions, our conjunctions, our phrases and clauses. The essence of the language is theirs.

What we have to do with this language is to take it as the common people have created it through the years—the speech we have known all our lives—and adapt it to the uses of our social level. We need not get into a dither about it; we need not frustrate ourselves and give it up as a bad job. We need to realize that so-called correctness is less significant than clearness if we are trying to get at what a man has to say, and that, after all, the way a man talks is less important than what he says.

No discussion of modern grammar can have much point if it disregards the speech of the masses of people who use it. Neither can it have much point if we separate it from the long line of tradition that is back of it. Our present grammar has a lineage many hundreds of years old. This is a fact that many persons have overlooked. Furthermore, interesting as comparisons are, and valuable too, we must remember—what many well-intentioned persons have not remembered—that English grammar cannot be thought of in terms of Latin grammar, and that only confusion and error can result from such a process.

----

*Broadside to the Sun, by Don West. W. W. Norton & Co., New York. By permission of the author.

The English language has its own history; and it has its own way of saying things, a way that can be understood in all its resourcefulness only as it rests on a knowledge of the sources from which modern English itself sprang.

2 An Incident and Its Implications

The young lieutenant closed the door briskly behind me. I had a moment to survey the room—large and terrifying in a way, with a thick carpet on the floor, heavy red velvet curtains at the windows, a massive crystal chandelier hanging from the ceiling, and at the far end an enormous desk, at which sat a stern-looking man perhaps fifty years old.

I walked slowly forward and spoke to him.

"I am here," I said as calmly as I could.

I saw the man's lips part in scorn. He motioned to me to sit down. He looked at me steadily. I waited for him to speak.

At last I said, "You sent for me."

"Yes." And he showed me an official envelope, smiling cruelly as he did so.

There was no need for me to read the inscription.

"This," he said, "is the order for your immediate arrest."

He turned back to the papers on his desk. He did not speak to me again.

I knew the interview was over.

The little scene you have just read has not been presented merely to whet your curiosity. It is intended as a dramatic illustration to show that words, gestures, expressions, and surroundings are all parts of a complex but unified set of conditions involving the process of communication between two people.

The room and the circumstances contributed something of

information to the person who entered there. The parting of the man's lips was full of meaning; his pointing to the chair was deliberate and intentional. His single word "Yes" was fearful in its implications as a reply to the sentence spoken to him. His final statement about the order, followed by his turning back to his desk, meant that the interview was ended.

The situation—the reactions of the men to each other, their facial expressions as they looked at each other, the movement of their hands and bodies, the words they spoke, the tones they used—cannot be separated from that particular place and that particular occasion as we try to re-create the scene in our imagination.

That is one reason why written words, even under the most favorable of conditions, often lead to misunderstandings. They are devoid of any indication of how they are to be read because the reader cannot know how the writer would have looked if he had spoken those words, or what the sound of his voice would have been. One can easily see why people sometimes travel great distances for the purpose of speaking to each other instead of sending a letter for the cost of an inexpensive postage stamp or of putting through a long distance call. One can understand also why the masses of people like plays and movies and television rather than books. In plays and movies and television the words are alive.

Facts, ideas, and emotions may be communicated by one person to another in a great variety of ways, some of them involuntary, some of them voluntary, many of them without the use of words. Direct as they are, however, facial expressions, gestures, and signs are all somewhat limited as a means of communication. I cannot convey any very complicated statement of my meaning, even in pantomime. I must use words arranged in some order to assist me because by comparison words so arranged are definite, and they offer greater possibilities as a means of conveying what I wish to convey.

Whether the communication is made intentionally or not, whether it is made with words or not, the fundamental requirement is that the communication be complete. If a man slams a door in my face, I know that he does not want to see me. My mind reacts: "That's that." If he tells me in a contract that he will pay me two hundred dollars a month to perform certain specified duties for him, I say to myself, "Well, I understand this business." I see how things are. The meaning is complete. Something inside me clicks.

Conditions vary greatly in the matter of communication. If a man addresses me in a foreign language, I cannot tell where one sentence ends and another begins. If a scientist shows me a complicated piece of laboratory apparatus and talks to me in a highly technical language, I cannot grasp his meaning. His words are lost on me. I cannot have any sense of completeness in any of his statements.

If, however, I and the person with whom I am speaking use the same language, if we employ pretty much the same words, if we have had rather similar experiences, and if we are of somewhat comparable intelligence, we may sooner or later end our efforts at communication with a realization that we have understood each other. Each has been able to grasp the other's statements as complete in themselves and as related to the other complete statements which made up the discourse.

In this book we shall have to presuppose that the reader has the ability to recognize a complete statement or question or command when one is put to him, whether the communication consists of one word or of many words. For if his mind cannot comprehend what is presented to him in the ordinary forms of communication, if he is irrational to the degree that he does not recognize a sentence when he hears one or reads one, then his study can do little for him. Then, however useful he may be as a citizen in his community, however upright he may be in his private and public dealings, he can never hope to accomplish much in the way of exact communication. He is psychologically and perhaps physiologically deficient in this respect. He can neither understand adequately what he hears or reads, nor tell another adequately what he has heard or read or experienced or felt. "In such cases," as the philosopher Kant once remarked, "men should devote their talents to other subjects."

3   What a Sentence Is

One day as I was walking down a street in a strange city I passed a large house set back on a spacious lawn. Suddenly I heard a woman's scream. I ran into the house as quickly as I could. There, on the floor, near the entrance, lay a young woman dead. She had been stabbed. Very soon other people began coming in just as I had come in.

My question is this: Why did I and those other people go into that house? All we had heard was a scream. Not a word had reached us. Why had we responded to a situation we knew nothing about?

The answer is that we did know something. We knew as plainly as we possibly could that a woman was mortally afraid.

This incident illustrates the most elemental fact of grammar: that exclamations—cries, shouts, and the like—which have their origin in emotion are the most primitive and universal forms of communication. A scream can be understood in any country in the world.

A scream is not a word in any conventional sense. No one can spell it or write it down on paper. It is simply an emotional sound made with the vocal chords. Now there are many emotional sounds, less violent, perhaps, than screams, cries, and shouts, which we attempt to represent as words. They have very

7

little meaning aside from the emotion they convey, but we spell them out and write them down. We use them sometimes by themselves: *Ouch!* Sometimes we use them with sentences: *No, I tell you I won't do it!* Sometimes we use them as substitutes for sentences: Who do you think you are, the president of the United States? *No, of course not!*

Some persons go so far as to say that these emotion words *(interjections)* are really sentences. Be that as it may, interjections have little or no meaning outside the emotional circumstance that called them forth. Consider swear words, for instance.

When a man builds a house he has to have a floor, walls, and a roof. He may put a rug on his floor and some pictures on his walls and some curtains at his windows after he gets his house built, but a floor, walls, and a roof are his absolute necessities. In the same way there are certain essentials in language if it is to rise above the situations represented by the emotion words we call interjections.

It is evident that we cannot say anything unless we have some thing or some idea to talk about. It is just as evident that we must have names for these things and ideas; for without names for them, we cannot talk about them. That is why we are always asking for the names of objects with which we are not familiar and for terms that represent ideas that are new to us. This, we are told, is an echelon lens. We do not actually know any more about an echelon lens than we did before. But we are satisfied because we now have a name for it that we can use if we want to tell anyone what we have seen or if we have some subsequent occasion for it. These words we call *nouns.* *

Useful though they are, name words by themselves cannot do much for us. We cannot go through life saying *bird, necktie, truth, beauty, goodness.* We must have some means—some other words—to tell us about these things and ideas, to tie them down, as it were, to make a statement about them, or to ask a

---

*In view of the uncertainty that still prevails regarding grammatical terminology, it seems to me wise, in most instances at least, to adhere to the traditional names.

question about them, or to give a command to someone about them.

Most of our talk is concerned with two purposes: to tell what something is like or what something does. To meet these needs we have two other kinds of words to go with our name words.

If we want to tell what something is like we use description words *(adjectives):*

Roses are red;
Violets are blue;
Sugar is sweet;
And so are you.

These statements are simple statements of qualities.

It often happens that we wish to make a different kind of descriptive statement, using a noun rather than an adjective. We tell what a word means by presenting it as a particular member of a general class: *The object is an echelon lens. The man is a soldier. The car is a Chevrolet. Taffy was a thief.* That is to say, Taffy was not the only thief; he was only one of the class of persons known as thieves. When we say *Taffy was a thief,* we assert that Taffy had the qualities we associate with thieves: *Taffy was thieflike.* To say that a certain car is a Chevrolet is to give it an identification, is to say that it has the characteristics which mark Chevrolets as distinct from other cars. We have given it an identification; in other words, a description.*

So much for these uses of language, either to tell what something is like or, which is much the same thing, to give it an identification, a classification. In both cases we are using description words: in the one case an adjective, in the other, a

---

*Most dictionary definitions are identifications of this kind. They have value only insofar as the hearer or reader is familiar with the terms used for the definition. If he doesn't know what a thief is, there isn't much use in telling him that Taffy is a thief. If, as frequently happens, he is not familiar with the definition term, he is obliged to look it up also, and so on, perhaps two or three times removed, until at last he comes upon a term the meaning of which is known to him. All this—whatever pains it may have cost —is only to express what is inherent in the word under scrutiny; it is not in reality to add anything new. The word and the definition are thus approximately equivalents.

noun. As a matter of fact they can both be called attribute words, attribute as I have used it, meaning to ascribe a quality or a classification.

Now, for the second kind of statement. If we want a word to tell what something does, we use a *verb*. Not all verbs are used to tell what something does, as we shall see later. But most verbs, aside from those used with description and identification words, are expressive of action or process:

> The mouse ran up the clock;
> The clock struck one;
> The mouse ran down.

Words expressive of change are extremely important words. As human beings we are much interested in events that take place around us, and in happenings that—so we believe—occur or have occurred in other times and in other places. Indeed our whole concept of time is only the record of change. If nothing ever happened, there would be no time.

Nouns, verbs, adjectives—name words, action words, description words representing these basic functions, as distinct from the emotional interjections—these are the three fundamental words in our language.

Fundamental as they are, however, they remain indefinite as long as they stand by themselves. It is only when we join two or more of them together that we can convey definite meanings. It is only when we say something specific about some specific thing that we have communication that is satisfying under the ordinary conditions of life. We can hardly be content to name an object without saying what it is like or what it does, and likewise we are not content to express an idea of action or quality without saying what object acts thus or has this quality.

We may have an idea conveyed by, say, *car,* and another idea conveyed by *go.* Each has its own meaning independent of the other. It is only when we put the two together that we give our communication specific meaning, when we discover and express a relationship between the idea of *car* and the idea of *motion:* "Car go." That was actually a child's first sentence. Putting two ideas together formed an expression of a pleasurable intellectual act. The child had put boundaries to his ideas by bringing them together into a tight relation, by making "hooked atoms" of them, as Epictetus might have said. When we have thus joined a name word either with an action word or with a description word or another name word, we have created a sentence.

Sentences created in this way are alike in that they say something in the *predicate* about something named in the *subject.* The subject and the predicate, each having its own content, are fused to make a statement; together they can do what neither could do separately. Such a fusion is comparable to that in chemistry where oxygen and hydrogen, each with its chemical characteristics, combine under certain conditions to form water, which, while it originates from oxygen and hydrogen, is not like either.

I have used the word *sentence* to represent the word structure I have been discussing as consisting of a subject and a predicate. It must be conceded, however, that the word *sentence* has been the subject of much debate. Some people limit it rather formally to the view that a group of words can be called a sentence only if it expresses a complete thought (Who is to say when a thought is complete?), with the implication that it is capable of standing alone. Such reasoning would exclude from the definition single words or groups of words which do not have a clearly identifiable subject and predicate, which do not—so it is said—express a complete thought, and which are not therefore capable of standing alone.

The issue between these views does not seem to me to be a matter of much significance. The important question is whether the words as they are used on a particular occasion are intelligible. You ask me whether I am going to town. I answer with a *Yes.* Under the circumstances the answer is clear. Am I walking or going in a car? *Walking.* You ask me where I left the book I was reading. *On the table.* Again the answers are clear and complete. What, then, is the difference between these expressions and those ordinarily and conventionally called sentences?

Insofar as a difference exists, it is perhaps in the degree to which the expression depends on related subject matter for its clearness. *The dog chased the cat,* as a statement, is clear by itself. Did the dog chase the cat? *Yes.* The answer is without meaning except as it is related to the question preceding it. *I do not like the plays of Shakespeare.* The comment that follows, *Neither do I,* is again entirely understandable and complete in this connection but meaningless if standing alone.

If the difference between these expressions and those with subject and predicate is of sufficient importance to justify a difference in terminology, it may be well to call them, by way of contrast, *sentences* and some such term as *sentence equivalents.* But I am not sure that even this distinction is altogether justifiable. For it is easy to point out that the same limitation I have been speaking of applies in some instances to what are unquestionably called sentences. It often happens that a sentence out of the blue is wholly unintelligible until its relations are explained. *So John bought the car after all.* After all *what?* What does *so* mean? The sentence doesn't say much in this case without a background. What had been said before? What would be said afterward? It would seem obvious that the term *sentence* cannot be limited to such structures as I described as having a subject and a predicate. What, then, does the word mean?

The science of linguistics can give an answer to this problem. Linguists have studied our speech and have discovered (what anyone could have discovered if he had stopped to think) that the way we say things is an important factor in our interpretation of language and in our concept of its grammatical structures. These scientists have pointed out the fact that spoken English involves not only differences between rising and falling stress patterns but also interruptions in our transition between the sounds that make up speech. They have discovered too that as a consequence of these characteristics of our speech there is a close relation between these characteristics and our grammatical structures. This is to say that the rhythm of English speech provides an important clue to its interpretation. That is, what the words mean in their relation one to another depends on how the words are said. *Yes,* with a period (.) and therefore a falling stress, means one thing, whereas *Yes,* with a question mark (?) and therefore a rising stress, means another thing. But in both cases there is in the manner of speaking an awareness that the utterance is complete—that it has reached a state of finality. Again, *Are we having fun,* with an exclamation mark (!), means one thing. *Are we having fun,* with a question mark (?), means another thing. Consider this: *The asparagus has been nice this year we have had much rain.* With a falling stress and a sufficient pause after *year,* the words form two sentences: *The asparagus has been nice this year. We have had much rain.* Without a falling stress and with only a slight pause after *year* we take the words as one sentence. *The asparagus has been nice this year, we have had much rain.* It may therefore be said that a sentence may be defined as consisting of those elements of discourse that are bounded by tone-pauses—thus distinct from whatever utterance may have preceded them and separated from whatever utterance may follow. This amounts, I suppose, to saying that a sentence consists of the utterances that fall between two silences. A definition thus stated resolves the distinction between *sentences* and *sentence equivalents,* being comprehensive enough to embrace them both.

4   Simple Sentence Patterns

S entences arise from a need to say something. What the need is will determine what kind of sentence is created. We can never understand or judge its value or effectiveness unless we can in imagination re-create the situation which called the sentence forth, unless we know the circumstances in which the sentence was originally spoken by somebody to somebody. These circumstances make up what is called the *context* of the sentence. Only as we know the context can we know fully what the sentence means.

Suppose I say this: *"The Yellow Dog was late."* Just that sentence by itself. You will understand every word in the sentence, but you will not understand what the sentence means. Now suppose that I have been reading to you Eudora Welty's charming little story "Delta Wedding," and that you have already learned that "Yellow Dog" is the nickname of a lazy train that meanders through Mississippi; then you will know at once what the sentence means. In fact, you will not even stop to think there could be any question of the meaning. This is what I have in mind when I say that the context of a sentence—the conditions which surround it—is essential to knowing what a sentence says.

We have seen that our needs for sentences are mostly (1) to tell what something does, (2) to tell what something is like, (3) to identify something as a member of a class. To convey these kinds of information we use different kinds of predicates: *verb predicates, adjective predicates, noun predicates.* The last two may be discussed under one heading as *attribute predicates,* being *predicates of quality* or *predicates of identification.*

VERB PREDICATES

Verbs express meanings but they do so under a variety of conditions. In a certain context the meaning expressed by a verb gives a sense of completeness; in another context it does not. The important fact is that when a verb is said to be complete in one context and incomplete in another, it is not really the same verb. The verb looks the same and it is pronounced in the same way, but the meanings are not the same. In *The rain stopped,* the verb does not have the same meaning as in *The man stopped the horse.*

We may go even further and say that no word has exactly the same meaning in any two sentences. There is a difference, for instance, between leaving one's home and leaving one's umbrella, though the expressions are identical in form; and eating soup is quite a different process from eating a piece of watermelon. The meaning of each word in a sentence depends partly on what the other words in the sentence mean. It is not, therefore, accurate to say that any particular verb may be called complete in one sentence and incomplete in another; nor is it accurate to say that some verbs are in themselves complete but that others are not, inasmuch as they are not really the same verb in two different contexts. Perhaps we can put the matter thus: Some contexts are such as to give the verb a sense of completeness, whereas some are not. *The context of the verb and not the verb itself is what makes it complete or incomplete.* *

Complete verbs are sentences in which the verb gives a sense of satisfaction in its completeness: *Birds fly. Canaries sing. The*

---

*Many grammarians call complete verbs *intransitive* verbs and incomplete verbs *transitive* verbs. I prefer the plainer definitions as being self-explanatory.

car won't go. The period in reading or the lowering of the stress
and the pause in speaking tells that the statement is complete.
These are two-part sentences, with the subject and the predicate in subject-predicate order. It may be worthwhile to remark that the number of such verbs is rather less than one
might suppose, as the most casual glance through a contemporary magazine will readily show.

Incomplete verbs are verbs of incomplete meanings; we feel
that they are incomplete because we need answers to questions
that the verbs have raised in our minds. What the questions are
and what the answers are will depend on the verbs and the circumstances.

Suppose that you and I were waiting for the weather to clear
before starting for a walk. Then we say this: *The rain stopped.*
The statement is complete in its context. But suppose, on the
other hand, that I am telling you about a runaway horse gallop-
ing down a street and that you are wondering what happened.
Then I tell you this: *A man stopped the horse.* In these circumstances to say *A man stopped* is to make a pointless remark.
But to say *A man stopped the horse* is to speak within the context of the sentence. It is obvious that *A man stopped* needs
completion. Stopped *what?* The word that tells the answer to
the question is called the *complement,* that which completes the
meaning.

Of the various kinds of complements which we are to discuss
in relation to verb predicates one much in use is that which
answers these questions: *What?* or *Whom?* For example: *The
girl dressed the doll. The dog chased the cat. The man stole the
money. The policeman caught the robber.* There are other complements as well. This answers the question of *when: The man
came yesterday.* This answers the question of *where: The boy
ran home.* There are others that may be roughly listed under
the heading of *extent:* How far? *The man walked a mile.* How
long? *The soldiers marched an hour.* How much? *The package
weighs a pound.* How fast? The car does eighty. One could perhaps think of others. There is still a third kind of complement.
To say *The man left* is not always to give adequate communica-

tion. Perhaps the manner of his leaving is the important element in the sentence. So, *The man left suddenly* is a satisfying remark. Again, in *The girl sings sweetly,* the manner of singing is more important than the mere act of singing.

These different kinds of complements are given different names. The *what* or *whom* complement is often called *the object;* the *when, where,* and *extent* complements are often called *adverbial objectives;* and the *thus* complement is simply an *adverb complement.* The difference in names doesn't mean a great deal, for in reality all complements are inherent in the verbs they complete. They are all actually *adverbs,* and the difference between them and adverb modifiers is very slight—the difference being that complements are rather more closely related to their verbs than adverb modifiers are, the object complement most closely of all. While complements complete the meaning of the verbs, as we say, they do so only because the meaning of the complement—like that of adverb modifiers—is contained within the meaning of the verb itself. For instance, the verb *went* implies the notion of some place to go: *The boy went home.* The verb *eat* implies the notion of something to be eaten: *The boy eats an apple.* And the verb *stop* implies the notion of a place of stopping: *The train stops here.* Complements, on the one hand, and adverb modifiers, on the other, are alike in this respect. It is therefore sometimes difficult to say whether a word is a complement or a modifier. As a matter of fact, the distinction is largely one of emphasis.

The sentences I have been talking about have a fundamental similiarity in that the subject precedes the verb. In a sentence with an incomplete verb the complement follows the verb, an exception being that adverb complements may, and often do, occupy a different position, as we shall see presently.

Subject, verb, complement—this word order is very important, especially with complements that answer the questions of *what* or *whom.* The word order in such a sentence is about the only way we have of knowing which noun is subject and which is complement. A simple illustration will make the matter clear. Let us take the following words: *The man beats the woman. The woman beats the man.* The words in the two sentences are exactly alike, and the sentences have exactly the same form. But in the sentence *The man beats the woman,* we know that it is the man who does the beating because the word *man* precedes the verb and is therefore recognized as the subject. We know also that it is the woman who is beaten by the fact that *woman* follows the verb, where we expect the complement to be. Even young children recognize this difference in position. If it is the woman who is doing the beating we are obliged to turn the sentence around: *The woman beats the man.* Under ordinary circumstances word order is the only way of keeping things straight. Language, like music, exists only in time. Once spoken, it ceases to be; we must grasp it as it comes.

The development of a conventional word order is a matter of considerable historical interest. A language like Latin depends for the interpretation of its sentences on the forms of its words and the changes they may undergo. Take three simple words: *puella, puer, amat,* meaning *girl, boy, loves.* By changing forms these three words can be made to say many different things. To write them as: *Puellam puer amat* means that the boy loves the girl, for *puellam,* though it comes first, has a complement form and is so recognized. To write the words as: *Puella puerum amat* is to say that the girl loves the boy, for *puella* is here a subject form and *puerum* is a complement form. This would be true even if the order were reversed: *Puerum puella amat,* for *puerum,* though it is first, is nevertheless a complement form. To change the form of the verb can produce still other sentences. *Puer puellam amabat* means that the boy *loved* the girl.

Old English, from which modern English came, was such an inflected language. Even before the Norman Conquest in 1066, however, there were evidences that a word order like ours was, not completely but partially, in use. For example (in literal translation): *Estonia is large very. He loved temperance. Then he the king visited. Was it then in every way a sad time.* (Note that the last sentence is not a question.)

When, after the Norman Conquest, Old English and Norman-French were brought into close contact, the old word endings gradually softened or completely disappeared. When the function of a word could no longer be determined by its form, some other method had to evolve. The simplest technique was that of position; so the subject was first and then the verb and then the complement—the word order we use today, the word order we recognize as natural and spontaneous, the word order we deviate from only for some special reason, a psychological order inasmuch as the subject is the first thing that comes to mind. To say *The boy chased the dog* is to speak conventional, meaningful English. To say *The dog the boy chased* is to leave the sentence wholly ambiguous. To say *The quickly corner turned the man* is to speak nonsense.

A language like Latin, which depends on word forms to indicate the uses of its words, is called a *synthetic* language. A language like English, which, as compared with Latin, is a relatively uninflected language—an *analytic* language as it is called —relies largely on context and position for its interpretation. (This is one reason why idiomatic English is a bit difficult for foreigners to learn.)

I have defined a complement as the word which gives an answer to a question raised by an incomplete verb, and I have pointed out that these questions and their answers are of various kinds. I wish now to remark that sometimes an incomplete verb may raise more than one question and consequently require more than one answer. Examples: *The boy saw the teacher yesterday. The man drove the car home. The man came home Friday. The child ate the candy ravenously.* As regards sentence order in such a case observe the following. If the sentence requires a *what* or *whom* complement, that complement immediately follows the verb and other complements follow it: *The man will buy a hat tomorrow.* If the sentence has a *when* complement, that complement will come last: *The man drove the car home yesterday.* An interesting fact about *when* complements and *adverb* complements is that they may be moved from their position as complements to other positions in the sentence, and thus not follow the verb and the object. For example: *Yesterday the man drove the car home. Tomorrow the man will walk a mile. Ravenously the child ate the candy.* These elements may likewise be shifted to follow the subject and precede the verb: *The man yesterday drove the car home. The child ravenously ate the candy.* In such shifts of position the words cease to be complements and become modifiers.

In my discussion I previously remarked that all complements are closely related to verb modifiers in that the meanings of complements are inherent in the meanings of the verbs to which they are related. But because some grammarians believe that adverbs are modifiers in whatever position they occur, I emphasize again my own belief that adverbs may and often do function as complements. For example: *The man spoke slowly. He left suddenly. He worked industriously.* I call *slowly, suddenly, industriously* adverb complements. To say that the man spoke is not in certain contexts complete to signify the circumstances of his speaking. To say *He spoke slowly* is to complete the meaning, to express something more than merely the fact of his speaking. Such sentences as these—with an adverb complement to complete their meaning—are much in use. An adverb may function as a complement even in a sentence which contains another complement: *The man read the book slowly.* I include within the category such sentences as these: *The girl wept bitterly. The man had walked far. The boy ran home quickly. The man struck the child angrily. The child spent the money hurriedly.* The question at issue is one of whether the adverbs are essential in those contexts. If the hearer or reader feels them to be essential, they are complements.

Although all complements thus far discussed answer questions raised by the verbs which precede them, the complements fall into two classes. Those which answer *what* or *whom* fall into one class; all the rest fall into the other. The important difference between the two classes is that the *what* and *whom* complements can be turned around and made into subjects, whereas the others can't. *The man spanked the baby* can become *The baby was spanked.* On the other hand we do not say *Home was went by the boy;* nor do we say *An hour was marched.* And to reverse the order of the sentence, *The man brought the car home Friday* does not transform either *home* or *Friday* into a subject. Only the *what* complement can be so transformed: *The car was brought home Friday.*

It sometimes happens, with verbs that demand an object, that the meaning under those particular conditions is still incomplete. We may say *The man painted the fence* and have complete meaning in certain contexts. But suppose the color of the fence is essential, after the fence is painted. Then we need further information. Let us say that the fence was white when the man got through with it. In such a case we add the word *white* to our sentence, putting it after the complement: *The man painted the fence white.* What we have done is to make *white* a part of the verb: The fence was *painted-white.* This means that *fence* is the complement of both *painted* and *white,* of what may be called a *discontinuous verb,* in reality a compound verb. *Goats don't mash the bucket flat;* that is: *Goats don't mash-flat the bucket.* Sometimes we use a noun in the same way as part of a compound verb: *The class elected John president.* What did the class do? It *elected-president* a boy named John. In modern English we make much use of sentences of this kind, in which an incomplete verb with an object absorbs an adjective or a noun to make a discontinuous verb.*

Before we leave the matter of verb predicates, we should take up briefly two topics not yet touched on. The first is that, though the chief purpose of verbs is to tell what something does, there are contexts in which the verb is not expressive of action at all. Take the sentences: *The man has a car,* or *The man owns a house.* In these no action is present. Nor is there any in *The house stood there a century.* The verb nevertheless takes a complement, and the complement is a *what* or *whom* complement. It may not be irrelevant to say that while no action is expressed, there is in some such cases an idea of action implied as having previously occurred. If the man has a car, he probably bought it; if the house stood there a century, it was because some per-

---

*In fairness to my reader I shall say that some grammarians simply make *white, flat* and *president* a second complement. I think the words are more vivid if they are thought of as parts of the verb.

son built it there. But the point here is that in these sentences, as stated, no present action is to be inferred. They may be called *verbs of inaction.* It is to be further noticed that with many such sentences the complement cannot be transformed into a subject. One may say *The house is owned by a man,* but we should scarcely say *A car is had by the man.*

The second and final matter is this: If a verb is to function as a predicate—whether of action *(I bought a car)* or of inaction *(I have a car)*—it must contain within itself the capacity to say something. For this reason such verbs are called *notional verbs;* this means that they have inherent meanings within the context in which they appear. In *I bought a car* the verb *bought* implies the act of purchase. In *I own a car* the verb *own* implies the sense of ownership. In both these sentences the verb, in contrast to those about to be discussed, carries the main weight of making an assertion. They are *notional verbs.*

ATTRIBUTE PREDICATES

Predicates made with adjectives and nouns are entirely different from those made with verbs. Verb predicates for the most part state actions, changes of some kind. Predicates made with adjectives and nouns for the most part ascribe a quality or an identification to the subject of the sentence. If one wishes to make a distinction, one may call them *description predicates* and *identification predicates.* In my discussion I shall treat them together. They are identical in form and closely related in meaning. In view of these facts I shall call them all *attribute predicates,* the word *attribute* meaning "ascribing quality or classification": *The paper is white. The book is a novel.*

In such sentences one could almost omit the word *is* altogether and put the predicate right next to the subject *(The paper— white. The book—a novel)* and still have a sentence. Children often use such verbless sentences: *Bobby hungry. Mimi tired. John sleepy.* Perhaps much of the early speech of children is of this kind. When a child says *dog* he probably means something like this: That thing I see is a dog. *Dog* is his predicate, his identification, his assertion about the object before him. *That* (is) *dog.* When he says *pretty* he no doubt means this: That object before me is pretty. *Pretty* comprises his assertion: *That* (is) *pretty.*

Sentences like these without any verb may be called by a rather formidable name: *appositional sentences.* The name isn't as bad as it sounds; it comes from a Latin word which means *placed next to.* An appositional sentence is so called because it contains no verb and its predicate is placed right next to the subject. The adjective or the noun (that is to say, the attribute) makes the statement about the subject, and so we may properly speak of them as *predicate adjectives* and *predicate nouns.* And we can appropriately put them both under the general term *attribute predicates.*

Appositional sentences, as independent sentences, have practically gone out of use in modern English; in fact they largely disappeared hundreds of years ago. But the combination of a noun with an attribute predicate is a useful element in many sentences even today: She stood before him, *her face tense with anger.* He wrote many poems, *some of them sonnets.* The beggars are coming to town, *some in rags, some in tags, some in velvet gowns.* It is necessary to remember this appositional form of structure for we shall meet it again in this chapter and in our later discussion of infinitives and participles.

Since in the appositional sentences which were in use in the early stages of development in our language, the predicate could be placed next to the subject, how does it happen that we today place a verb between the subject and the predicate? The answer is very simple.

Let us look at a sentence: *The man ill.* We learn the fact of the illness, but we do not know when it occurred or even whether it actually occurred. The trouble is that a verbless appositional sentence has no power to answer these questions for us, for very few adjectives or nouns are capable of indicating time or other circumstance. A most satisfactory remedy was found for this difficulty. The old verb *be* was once a complete verb, as in sentences like these: *God is. Carthage is no more.* A few of these still remain. But generally the verb became devoid of content. The interesting fact, however, is that, though it lost its meaning and ceased to be a notional verb, it still kept its power to express tense. Hence we can say such things as these: *The man is ill* (present). *The man was ill* (past). The use of *be* as a verb between the subject and the attribute predicate was a clever device and has remained so down to the present day. The old appositional sentences still kept their vivid predicate adjectives and nouns and at the same time were enabled to indicate tense.

The forms of *be* help merely to convey that the information expressed by the predicate is meant to be taken at face value, as true or as not true: *The man is ill.* or *The man is not ill. The dogs are greyhounds.* It often happens, however, that a given statement is not meant to be taken for a fact, is not meant as a downright statement: *The book may be a novel. Children should be kind.* In these two sentences other verbs have been added to the verb *be* to help it out in giving various shades of meaning we may wish to convey—not that the book *is* a novel but that it *may be;* not that children *are* kind but that they *should be.*

Such helping verbs are called *auxiliaries.* They are a very important group: *can, could, may, might, shall, should, will, would, must, do, have,* and some others, like *dare* and *need.* We shall have more to say of auxiliaries later in the discussion of the infinitive, where their use is altogether different from that under discussion here. Now we are noticing only that they can help in expressing more shades of meaning than can be expressed by *be* alone, which expresses only tense. "Shades of meaning" are what grammarians define as *mode.* For this reason the auxiliaries are sometimes called *modal auxiliaries.* *

In addition to the verb *be* and its auxiliaries there are certain other verbs which may be used with description or identi-

---

*In speaking of these words as auxiliaries I recognize the merit in the remark sometimes made that inasmuch as they are avowedly helping words they should be spoken of as modifiers of the verb *be* rather than as verbs proper. This is to say that they might better be called adverbs. Whatever they are called, their function is clear.

fication predicates to make statements that are not meant as
out-and-out assertions. The verb *be* makes or denies a flat
statement: *The man is a soldier. The man is not a soldier.* The
verbs I am speaking of, like the modal auxiliaries, make quali-
fied statements: *The boy seems ill. The woman looks tired. The
man acts like a fool.* Such verbs are very useful. They enable us
to say not that a statement is or is not true, but that it has the
appearance of being or of not being true. I am not saying that
the boy is ill or that the woman is tired or that the man is a fool,
but that they have the appearance of being so, although they
may not be. Such verbs, to the extent that they express the idea
of possibility, are to that extent notional verbs.

Verbs like *looks, seems, feels* (in such situations as I have
presented) have more meaning than the forms of *be,* but nevertheless the responsibility for the assertion is still on the attribute predicate. There are many other verbs too, with still
more meaning, that may be used with predicate adjectives and
nouns: *The girl stood still. The weeds grew tall. Henry Jones
became mayor.* When such verbs are used with attribute predicates, they are different from those same verbs used as predicates in other sentences. As predicates they are asserting verbs:
The weeds grew. In the sentence I have used *(The weeds grew
tall.)* the verb *grew* is not the predicate; the adjective *tall* is the
predicate. It is not the fact that the weeds grew that is significant, but the fact that *they became tall by growing.*

Verbs like all these we have been discussing (as *be, seem,
grew,* which come into an appositional sentence, that is, which
come between the subject and the predicate adjective or noun)
may be called *complementary verbs.* They help out (complete)
the attribute predicate by giving it tense or other circumstance.

I emphasize the importance of the term *attribute predicate*
because I believe it states exactly what function the adjective or
noun here fulfills—that of predicate—just as in the previous
section I emphasized the function of the verb as predicate, remembering that verb predicates consist of notional verbs, that
is, verbs with inherent meaning, whereas complementary verbs
serve only as aids to the more important attribute predicate. I

therefore propose the following as the formula for the sentences
I have just been discussing: subject, complementary verb, attribute predicate.

I have now to discuss two sentence forms that are based on
the formula I have presented, but that are more complex, involving as they do the discussion of both verb predicates and
attribute predicates.

For the first of these I give two sentences that are closely
related: *The boy left town a pauper. The man came home a
millionaire.* In such sentences we use for the complementary
verb not a form of the verb *be* or even of a modal auxiliary
combined with *be,* but a more complicated structure. It may be
observed that the complementary verb in this sentence is made
up of a notional incomplete verb followed by a complement, the
whole functioning as a complementary verb. When the boy left
town, he was in the class known as a pauper—that was his identification; when as a man he came home he had the station of a
millionaire—that again was his identification. The facts that he
was at one time a pauper and that at a later time he was a
millionaire are the significant facts that the two sentences mean
to convey, rather than the facts that he left town and later came
home. *Pauper* and *millionaire* are the predicates. Sentences of
this kind are relatively rare.

There is still another kind of sentence that makes use of the
attribute predicate: *The man found the child ill.* This sentence
obviously is unlike *The man painted the fence white,* for it is
evident that the child was not ill as a consequence of the man's
finding it in the way that the fence was white as a result of the
man's painting it. Neither is it like *The boy left town a pauper,*
in which *pauper* is the predicate making a statement about the
boy. In the sentence *The man found the child ill* we are using
child as the subject of *ill.* What was it the man discovered? *The
child was ill.* Here we have a survival of the old appositional
structure we talked about, with the attribute predicate placed
smack up against the subject. *The man found the child ill. The
woman thought the girl a liar. Child* is the complement of *found*
and the subject of *ill; girl* is the complement of *thought* and the

subject of *liar.* We shall meet this sentence when we come to the study of the infinitive. And we shall discover also that this kind of sentence is closely related to the complex sentence with a noun clause for an object.

SUMMARY

The description of the complementary verb concludes our discussion of the two kinds of predicate in the three simple patterns that are the basic patterns of all English sentences. We must remember that it is the way it is used, and not the verb itself, which determines whether it is complete or incomplete or complementary. By way of illustration consider the following sentences:

- Complete verb: *The wind blew.*
- Incomplete verb with various complements:

> What complement: *The wind blew the curtain.*
> When complement: *The wind blew yesterday.*
> Extent complement: *The wind blew a gale.*
> Adverb complement: *The wind blew furiously.*

- Complementary verb: *The door blew shut.*
- Discontinous verb: *The wind blew the door shut.*
- Appositional structure used as complement: *The man found the door blown shut.*

ILLUSTRATIONS

The following little stories illustrate the simple sentence patterns that have made up the subject matter of this chapter:

Jack Spratt was a man. Jack Spratt had a wife. Jack could not eat fat. The wife could not eat lean. The lean kept Jack lean. The fat made the wife fat. Jack grew leaner. The wife became fatter. Jack licked the platter clean. The wife cleared the table.

Mother Hubbard was old. Mother Hubbard had a dog. Mother

Hubbard had a cupboard. The dog was hungry. The dog wanted a bone. Mother Hubbard did not have a bone. Mother Hubbard found the cupboard empty. The dog went hungry. Mother Hubbard felt sad. The dog howled loudly.

Simple Simon met a pieman. The pieman sold pies. Simon wanted a pie. The pieman wanted a penny. Pies cost money. Simon did not have a penny. Simon did not get a pie. The pieman left suddenly. Simple Simon was unhappy.

5   Simple Modifiers

The little stories you have just read at the end of the last chapter show how limited bare sentences are. They can make statements but they lack the interest that comes from details of description and circumstance. Even though we have great numbers of nouns, verbs, adjectives, and adverbs with which to form the basic structures of the English sentence, we have many things to say that cannot be said by these words alone. There is a simple way of supplementing this basic vocabulary. This is the use of modifiers. Modifiers are of various kinds: simple adjectives and adverbs and the more complex adjective and adverb phrases and clauses. In this chapter we shall discuss only the simple forms.

COMPOUNDS

One way of enriching our sentences is to use compound words, a way that has been used for centuries. Old English made much use of compound terms: *swan way, whale path, shield wall.* We make many compounds of nouns, for example, placing one name word in front of another. Thus we say *boxcar,* a railway car built like a box, a descriptive compound; *railway* is itself a compound, a way made of rails; or we make use of a compound of material, like *sandpile,* a pile composed of sand. And we have *sunrise,* where *sun* is the subject of *rise; armchair,* a descriptive compound, a chair with arms. We scarcely think of such nouns as two words for we are familiar with them as one. We hardly think of them as compounds even when they are written separately: *coal miner,* where *coal* is the complement of *miner,* its subject; or *woman hater,* again where *woman* is the complement of *hater,* a woman who is hated by someone.

In these expressions the first noun is a modifier of the second. Thus compound nouns are much like nouns with adjective modifiers. For example, *red* can be the name of a color: *Red is a warm color.* But when we find it preceding a noun—interpretation by position—we say that *red* is an adjective, a modifier. One could as well say *The man has redhair* as *The man has red hair,* for *red hair* is only a descriptive compound, hair that is red, just as *armchair* is a chair with arms. This is to say that a noun preceding another noun makes a construction much like that of a noun with a modifying adjective and is often indistinguishable from it.

I said earlier that a *boxcar* was a certain kind of *railway* car. Now *railway* is itself a compound. Is it a noun or an adjective? I confess that I can't think it very important what we call it. It is a modifier in any case. The significant fact is not the name but the frequent use we make of such multiple compounds: *railway boxcar, an air mail postage stamp, an economy class airplane ticket,* and dozens of others—*a ninety-cent three-way light switch.*

All the compounds thus far presented have been composed of name words joined together. Now I speak of another kind of compound composed not of two or more name words joined together but made up of whatever assortment seems to fulfill our need. Here are some illustrations: The sun, let us say, is beginning to shine through the clouds. Query—Is this a *clear-up* or a *breakthrough?* Next: I had hoped for a *cutback* on the deal. Last: This is my *day off.* We have no hesitation about making such combinations as suit us. It can truly be said that compounds of any kind are *shortcuts* to eliminate more wordy discourse at the same time that they enrich our vocabulary.

Verbs too are often compounded, sometimes written as one word: *The court upheld the decision.* They are sometimes written as separate words: *The robbers held up the bank.* Sometimes they are discontinuous verbs: *The boy held the book up.* Often, though not always, as in the sentences I have used for illustration, the meaning of the compound changes from one use to another.

I wish to call attention to the last sentence, for it illustrates an important fact that is often misunderstood. *The boy held the book up* is like the German construction of a verb with what is called a separable particle: *We go the stairs up.* In English this becomes: *We go up the stairs.* *Up* in such a sentence is not a preposition as it is sometimes said to be but a part of the compound verb—which is to say this: The court's decision must be *upheld,* where *up* is clearly neither a preposition nor an adverb. The fact that *up* is part of the verb can be seen in the following sentence: *We must the stairs up-go.* We make much use of such verbs. For example: *We brought the apples in,* in which *in* is an integral part of the verb: *We brought-in the apples.*

I have already discussed verbs with adverb complements: *The man left suddenly.* Here are some examples of verbs with what might be mistaken for adverb complements: *The girl came in,* in which *in* is not an adverb complement but a part of the verb meaning *entered.* Likewise, in *The child fell down,* and *The man sat down, down* does not tell where the man sat or where the child fell, but what the man and the child did. The point is that, though these compounds are made up of verbs and adverbs, the adverbs are neither complements nor modifiers, but genuine parts of a compound verb.

Compound adjectives and adverbs may be disposed of quickly. Consider, for example, the following: *a two-edged sword, a three-legged stool, a far-reaching decision, a well-kept lawn.* These examples are made of a participle modified by an adverb. But this is not always the case: *The man was completely down and out.* Here are some compound adverbs: *to and fro, now and then, up and down, in and out, nowadays.*

This discussion of compounds, meager as it is, is perhaps enough to suggest the extent to which the resourcefulness of the English language can be indefinitely increased.

MODIFIERS

Another way of helping out our English vocabulary, in addition to creating compounds, is to use modifiers.

Adjective Modifiers

We have already discussed predicate adjectives. Here we are to speak of adjectives as they may be joined to nouns in the form of modifiers.

A predicate adjective is used to make a statement about its subject: *The bird is blue.* A compound identifies a particular kind of bird: *A bluebird is small,* referring to a certain small bird with a pinkish breast. When we say *The boy saw a bluebird,* we know that the boy saw a particular kind of bird. But when we say *The boy saw a blue bird,* we may refer to any kind of bird that is blue, the only limitation being that of color. Adjectives as modifiers do not make statements about the nouns they modify, nor do they limit the nouns to a particular class. But they make the nouns more definite than they would be without the modifier. When we say *The boy saw a bird,* we only differentiate *bird* from other kinds of living creatures. When we say *The boy saw a blue bird,* we limit our meaning to birds that are blue. *Red* birds, *yellow* birds, and *green* birds do not enter the mind. And when we say *The boy saw a bluebird,* we have limited our meaning still further. The process of modifying is therefore a process of exclusion.

In contrast to predicate adjectives, which occupy a position after the complementary verb (The children *were happy.*), adjectives as modifiers are placed directly with the nouns they modify. And, like the first element in a compound noun, they usually precede their noun: The *happy children* were singing.

Adjectives indicate quality or quantity: The man is *old.* The

man has *much* money. They may modify nouns in any of the
uses of nouns that we have studied: subject, complement, or
predicate. The following little story illustrates these uses:

> An old woman had a little basket. The basket contained four
> fresh eggs. The eggs were large, white eggs. The old woman
> dropped the little wicker basket. The beautiful eggs broke.

These short sentences show important differences in the uses
of adjectives. In the first sentence we have two adjectives, one
modifying the subject (*old* woman) and one modifying the object (*little* basket). In the second sentence we have two adjectives—one of quality and one of quantity *(fresh* and *four)*. The
adjectives modify the same noun but they are not of equal rank.
There were fresh eggs and there were four of them. *Fresh* modifies *eggs* and *four* modifies *fresh eggs.* No comma is used between such adjectives. On the other hand, in sentence three we
have adjectives of equal rank, both modifying *eggs (large, white*
eggs). These are called *coordinate adjectives,* and they are separated by commas. In the fourth sentence (The old woman
dropped the little wicker basket.) we have two adjectives of
quality (*old* and *little),* one modifying the subject and the other
modifying the object. The word *wicker* as here used is not an
adjective but a noun, a part of the compound noun *wicker
basket.* The two words *little* and *wicker* are not separated by
commas for *little* modifies *wicker basket.* In the last sentence
(The beautiful eggs broke.) we have an adjective of quality
modifying the subject of the complete verb.

The usual position for an adjective modifier is to precede its
noun. Sometimes, however, in writing—but seldom in speech—
we place an adjective after its noun. To do so is to change is
meaning and to some extent its effect, in that such a position
slows down the movement of the description and causes the adjective to approximate the function of a predicate adjective.
One almost feels the presence of a verb: *The night,* (it was) *dark
and silent, overtook the man.* Joseph Conrad makes much use
of this placing of the adjective. In his story "The Lagoon," we
find this: "The forests, *somber and dull,* stood motionless and

silent on each side of the broad stream." And again: "A cry
discordant and feeble skipped along the smooth water." Sometimes a single adjective follows its noun to make a compound
word: *sum total, court martial.* This is probably due to French
influence. But an adjective following its noun seldom stands
alone. Either there are two or more adjectives or the adjective is
modified by a phrase: *The man, miserable in his defeat, left the
field.*

Adverb Modifiers

English adverbs are of two kinds: those that end in *-ly* and
those that do not. Examples of the former are: *suddenly, angrily, quickly;* examples of the latter: *in, near, far, then, still, why,
when.* Some adverbs use both forms, often with different meanings. In *The kite flies high, high* is the complement of *flies,* as
contrasted with *The men think highly of the arrangement,*
where *highly* fuses with *think* to form a compound verb
equivalent to *esteem.* For *The boy ran madly down the street,*
we can also say this: *The boy ran like mad down the street.*

The adverbs ending in *-ly*—and we have hundreds of them—
have been formed from adjectives of quality to become adverbs
of manner (sometimes called *thus* adverbs): *quiet, quietly; angry, angrily.* The *-ly* comes from Old English *-lic,* which is preserved in our modern *like. The boy went quiet-like—The boy
went quietly. The boy spoke anger-like—The boy spoke angrily.*
In this connection we still use an expression with *like* in instances in which no adverb ending in *-ly* has ever been formed:
The boy ran like a deer. The boy ran like lightning. In such
cases we use a prepositional phrase, as we shall see in the next
chapter. We have never made an adverb *deerily* or *lightningly,*
for we do not make an adverb by adding *-ly* to a noun.

The business of adverbs, it is usually said, is to modify verbs,
adjectives, and other adverbs. But the matter is not so simple as
such a statement would lead one to believe. For one thing, an
adverb that is used to modify another adverb is of a very special
kind, as will be discussed later in this chapter. For another

thing, an adverb does not actually modify an adjective, inasmuch as an adjective modified by an adverb is a participle, a verbal adjective; and it is the verbal aspect rather than the adjectival aspect that is modified by the adverb: *The woman wore a richly embroidered scarf.* The scarf was richly embroidered because someone had previously performed the act of embroidering it. In *You should use finely chopped vegetables, chopped* not only describes the vegetables but implies as well that someone had done the chopping. More often than not such adverbs modify the past participle, but sometimes they modify the present participle: *I saw them in a rapidly whirling dance. The decision will have far-reaching consequences.*

The statement that adverbs modify verbs is not so simple as it sounds. In discussing the patterns of English sentences, I pointed out that adverbs are sometimes so essential to the interpretation of a sentence as to be complement rather than modifier: *The child wept bitterly. The man had walked far.* And, I said, even with a verb which requires an object an adverb may serve as a complement. I cited some examples: *The man struck the child angrily. The child spent the money hurriedly.* The test I proposed was one of whether the adverb was essential to the meaning of the sentence in its particular context. And I remarked that in some cases it would be difficult to say whether the adverb was actually essential as a complement or accessory as a modifier, it being a matter of how much emphasis one wishes to put on the adverb. In spoken rather than in written discourse such confusion is not likely to occur.

The relation between a verb and an adverb is sometimes so close that the verb absorbs the adverb and makes it a part of itself, as we saw when we were speaking of compound verbs: *uphold, come in, withstand, sit down, overcome.* Often the meaning is changed in the process, for *uphold* does not mean *hold up* and *overcome* does not mean *come over.*

Ordinarily an adverb does not come between a verb and its complement. But if the adverb is short or if the complement has a long modifier, the adverb may immediately precede or follow the verb: *The foolish child soon spent the money. The man car-*

ried out successfully his arduous task in the Far East. The adverb in a sentence with a complementary verb may occur almost anywhere: *John is a general now. John is now a general. The child is usually well.* Also, in a sentence with a complementary verb, the adverb is usually a modifier of the entire predicate. Once in a while the adverb occurs at the opening of the sentence. Such sentences are placed out of their natural order for purposes of emphasis. To say *Suddenly the ball smashed the window* is more emphatic than to say *The ball smashed the window suddenly,* where the adverb would ordinarily be placed last: subject, verb, object, adverb complement. This device for giving emphasis is easily overworked. Many books for children use it quite to the distortion of the English sentence order: *Quickly Jim ran down the street. Away ran Johnny.* This is done to create an artificial sense of excitement.

Adverbs do not always modify one single word in a sentence, but sometimes as *sentence modifiers* they modify the whole sentence: *Obviously, the man was insane. The girl, unfortunately, had no home. The effect was disastrous, certainly.* Such modifiers may occur in various positions and are set off by commas. In general, adverbs are far more flexible as to position than adjectives are. This distinction is sometimes carried much further than I have suggested here, namely that variableness in position is the characteristic that distinguishes adverbs from the fixed-position adjectives.

There is a class of words that are often given the name of *adverbial objectives;* but the adverbial objectives are nothing more than the complements we have already met in our study. They are the *when, where,* and *how much* complements we have discussed. Many times such words modify other adverbs, often expressing time: *The man left an hour ago.* Often they modify adjectives, nearly always expressing space: *John is six feet tall.* Sometimes they modify nouns: *The road home is rough. The journey inland is dangerous. The work there taxed the community.*

There is a group of words that are always called adverbs. They are not, however, really adverbs, for they do not add to or enrich the meanings of the words they are attached to. They merely intensify those meanings. They may be called *intensives*. They may be used almost anywhere in a sentence: *The day is very warm. Only John must go. The children have just come in. It was only two o'clock. John has only a dollar. The man very often lies. The man is very sick.* Many swear words are intensives.

ILLUSTRATIONS

Good King Arthur ruled the land. King Arthur was a goodly king. The King stole barley meal. The King made a bag pudding. The King stuffed the pudding well. The King used only ripe plums. The King used much fat. The pudding tasted good. The pudding was very large. The King could not devour the pudding that night. The next morning the Queen fried the scraps.

Once a lion was asleep. A little gray mouse ran by. The lion awoke. The lion caught the little mouse. The lion spoke loud words. The little mouse was badly frightened.

"I meant no harm. You should spare my life."

The lion smiled. He lifted his big, heavy paw. The mouse scampered away.

Later the lion was ranging the woods. He was stalking his prey. A trap snared the lion. He was frightened.

"I can never escape."

The lion thrashed about hopelessly. He roared. His roar filled the jungle.

The little mouse heard the roar. He came quickly. He saw the big lion. The mouse nibbled the thick ropes. He got the lion free. The lion thanked the mouse. The mouse was happy.

"One good turn deserves another."

6   Prepositional Phrases

The adverbs that do not undergo inflection (*then, here, still, before*), the prepositions, and the conjunctions are all called *particles*. Adverbs do not require complements: *I have been here before.* Prepositions require complements: *I came before noon.* Conjunctions also require complements: *I left before he came.* In this chapter we are concerned with prepositions.

A prepositional phrase is composed of a preposition with a noun or pronoun or another phrase or a clause as its complement. Phrases are used as adjectives or as adverbs or, less frequently, as nouns. The number of prepositions in English is very large—approximately three hundred—and so the uses of prepositional phrases aid greatly in the expression of meanings too complicated to be stated by simple adjectives, adverbs, verbs, and nouns, as can be seen from the illustrations at the end of the last chapter.

An example here will show the great variety of meanings that can be expressed merely by a change of preposition. Let us take three words: *man, is, house.* Then we can say something like this: *The man is in the house. The man is near the house. The man is behind the house. The man is under the house. The man is on top of the house.* And we could go on. Prepositions express relationships; each relationship has its own shade of meaning.

Prepositions and adverbs are closely related. Adverbs have no complement: *The accident had occurred before.* This is to say that this was not the first occurrence. If we wish to say that the accident had occurred before a specified time we add a complement: *The accident had occurred before noon.* When we add a complement to an adverb, we transform the adverb into a preposition. It is interesting that adverbs which end in *-ly* do not become prepositions. Nor, it should be added, do some other adverbs: *here, there, far, still.*

The language used in England before the Norman Conquest in 1066, and by the common people for a long time afterward, was, as I discussed in an earlier chapter, an inflected language. Its words changed form to indicate their uses. In this way it was possible, for instance, to show whether a noun was a subject or a complement or a modifier. In the years of confusion that followed the coming of the Normans many changes occurred. Two peoples speaking different languages naturally met the problem as best they could. The development of a recognized word order (subject, verb, complement) did much to make those word relations clear. No doubt the changes worked in both directions. The development of a word order made the inflections no longer essential, and the loss of the inflections made the evolution of a word order all the more necessary. But the recognition of an accepted word order within the sentence did not altogether make up for the loss of the inflections, especially of the old nouns in the genitive and dative cases. And so this development was accompanied by the development of prepositions in greater and greater numbers to make word relationships unmistakable. In fact, the use of prepositions has more than made up for the loss of the ancient inflections because they can convey more numerous and more accurate relationships.

Having seen briefly why prepositional phrases developed, we may now with equal brevity inquire into their origin. Let us look at a sentence containing a prepositional phrase: *John is working in the yard.* In such a sentence *in* would originally have been an adverb, just as it is in this instance: *John is staying in today. The yard* would have been a noun in the dative case with an inflectional ending, also modifying the verb. The noun *the yard* was placed right after the adverb *in* (appositive to it, placed next to it) to explain what was meant by *in*, to tell where *in* was. Then, because the adverb preceded the noun (was prepositional to it, that is, placed before it), the adverb and the noun were fused into a unit, a phrase, with *in* as the preposition and *the yard* as its complement. Once the phrase was formed as a unit, it became extremely useful, especially as it could be shifted to other positions in the sentence.

The most common use of the prepositional phrase is to modify a noun or a verb: *A little girl was walking in the woods. The name of the little girl was Red Ridinghood. She was carrying a basket of food to her grandmother. Red Ridinghood met a wolf in the woods near her grandmother's house.* Prepositional phrases have other uses as well:

- As predicate: *The dress was of silk. The book was on the table. The house seemed in good condition.*
- As part of a discontinuous verb: *The shock put the girl to bed.*
- As an appositional predicate: *John found the house in good condition.*
- As modifier of an adjective: *An old man, terrible in appearance, came in.*
- As complement of an adjective: *John was eager for success.*
- As complement of a noun: *John had a great desire for wealth.*
- As complement of a preposition: *The man came from behind the house.*
- As subject: *Over the fence is out.*
- As complement of a verb: *Charles worked for success.*

Some prepositional phrases, like some adverbs, may modify a whole sentence rather than a specific word within the sentence: *On the whole, John was fairly efficient. The man, even under supervision, was not a good workman. John was not a bad boy, for all his faults.* Such modifiers, like adverbial sentence modifiers, are set off by commas. Like single words, prepositions and prepositional phrases are often modified by intensives: *The children heard the alarm just before noon. The men are free only on Saturday nights.* Many prepositions are compounds—made up of two or more phrases: *The man stood in front of the house. I will do this because of my friendship for you. In accordance with the plan I shall leave at once.*

The eighteenth century promulgated a principle that a sentence should never end with a preposition—a battle cry that has been sounded vociferously ever since. Such a rule violates one of the essential characteristics of the English language and consequently has no validity whatsoever. It overlooks the fact that English verbs often assimilate an adverb. In *The car turned over,* for example, *turned over* is the verb phrase. Likewise a verb may assimilate a preposition to make a verb phrase with an object: *The girl went up the stairs. The goat walked over the bridge.* Here *went-up* and *walked-over* are verb phrases. Often the use of such a verb phrase demands that the phrase be broken up into a discontinuous verb, with the so-called preposition at the end of the sentence. *The girl sent for the doctor* may become *The doctor was sent for* or *What are you aiming at?* Or again, to quote Robert Browning: *"I was the man the Duke spoke to."*

In this legitimate use of a so-called preposition at the end of a sentence English resembles its related language—German, with its "separable particles," which are not really prepositions at all. For example, one would not say this in German: *I go up the stairs.* He would say this: *I go the stairs up.* That *up* is not a preposition can be seen in a sentence like this: *I must the stairs up-go.* In current usage, and by historical precedent, there is no foundation for the rule. Hence one may say this: *What did you do that for?*

ILLUSTRATIONS

A hare was always boasting about his speed. "I can run very fast. No one will race with me."

None of the other animals would race with the hare. Finally

the tortoise spoke up. "I will race with you." He spoke slowly in a low voice.

The hare laughed at the tortoise. The animals looked surprised. The tortoise was the slowest of the animals. The hare was very gay. He was not anxious about the outcome of the race with the tortoise.

"This is a good joke. I can beat you in a few minutes."

The animals arranged the race for the next day.

The animals watched the race in great glee. They made fun of the slow old tortoise.

The hare started off with great speed. The hare looked back of him. He could not see the tortoise anywhere on the road.

The hare lay down in the shade of a big tree. The warm day made the hare sleepy. He slept in the shade of the tree for a long time.

During this time the tortoise was plodding along the road. He moved very slowly. After about an hour he passed the hare. He crawled past without a sound.

The hare finally woke up with a start. He saw the tortoise ahead of him. The tortoise was just finishing the race.

The animals cheered the tortoise with loud voices. The hare had lost the race by his carelessness. He could never again boast about his speed.

7 Inflection

The discussion thus far has limited itself to the basic structures of simple sentences, with their modifiers. Nothing has been said about changes in the forms of the words that make up these basic sentences.

The uses of words in simple sentences have been illustrated many times in the preceding pages. It cannot be overemphasized that any word used in any one of these structural functions thereby acquires the characteristics of that function. If I say *I see a man,* I have used *man* as a noun; but if I say *The lifeguards man the boats,* I have used *man* as a verb. If I use *man* as a noun, I must consider its grammar as a noun; I may wish to know how it forms its plural. If I use it as a verb, I must consider its grammar as a verb; I may wish to know how it forms its past tense.

Old English was an inflected language, but the word *inflection* is almost an anomaly in modern English. If it were not for a very few words—mostly the verb *be* and the personal pronouns—we could almost get along without any mention of inflection. Modern English comes very close to being a non-inflected language; that is, it has very few changes in the forms of its words to show their interpretation in a sentence.

What few inflections survive from pre-Conquest days—only

two major inflections—can be discussed as they pertain to a few
so-called basic rules of grammar.

THE MATTER OF AGREEMENT

We have seen that usually a sentence is a two-part structure
consisting of a subject and a predicate. Now one of the most
commonly stated rules of grammar is that the subject and the
predicate agree in number and person. The rule thus given out
implies that words used as subjects and as verbs have some
power of indicating number, that is, of showing whether the sentence pertains to one (*singular*) or to more than one (*plural*) and
of indicating person, that is, of showing whether the sentence
pertains to a speaker (*first person*) or to a person addressed
(*second person*) or to a person or thing spoken of (*third person*).
We shall discuss this statement under the two headings of
number and person. We shall thus learn to what extent these
implications are limited.

Number

Except for a few words (like *sheep* and *deer*) English nouns
are capable of distinguishing singular and plural number. They
do so—about ninety-five percent of them—by adding -*s* or -*es* to
the singular to make the plural: *tree, trees; horse, horses;
church, churches; baby, babies; monkey, monkeys.* Many
nouns which formerly made their plurals in other ways now use
the regular ending, and practically all nouns coming into the
language employ this method. Two kinds of nouns form their
plurals differently. There are, first, certain English nouns
which have survived from earlier times: *man, men; mouse,
mice; foot, feet.* And there are, second, certain nouns from foreign languages which have retained their foreign plurals:
seraph, seraphim; beau, beaux; alumnus, alumni. Many of the
old irregular English nouns have developed or are developing
regular plurals in -*s* or -*es: eye, eyes* instead of *eyen; shoe, shoes*
instead of *shoon;* and foreign nouns often develop regular plu-

rals: *index, indexes* instead of *indices; cherub, cherubs* instead
of *cherubim.* In whatever way the plural is formed, whether
regularly or irregularly, the generalization which says that *the
ability of nouns to distinguish singular from plural is one of the
two almost universal inflections remaining in the English language* is sound. German, in contrast to English, has complicated
ways of forming plurals of nouns, which make for considerable
difficulty in learning German. Spanish, on the other hand, has
gone much further than English in this regard, for Spanish plurals are regular in their endings in *-s.*

As regards pronouns the matter is different. Certain pronouns do not have the power to distinguish number: *What is
this book? What are these books? Which of you is going? Which
of you are going? Who is the man? Who are the men?* On the
other hand *this* and *that* have plurals: *This is mine. These are
yours. That is mine. Those are yours.* By contrast, the personal
pronouns are complicated in their inflection. They can indicate
not only number but case as well (the function of the pronoun
within the sentence, whether as subject or as object, for example). With reference to agreement of subject and predicate,
which is the matter under discussion, we have these forms for
the singular: *I, you, he, she, it;* for the plural we have these: *we,
you* (indistinguishable from the singular) and *they.**

The difficulty involved in the rule of agreement between subject and predicate is that whereas verbs retain their power to

---

*The lack of distinction between *you* as singular and *you* as plural is similar to that in
German, where the singular and plural of *Sie* must be determined by context: *Haben Sie
ein Buch?* (Have you a book?). One cannot say whether one person or more than one is
being addressed, *Sie* as a second personal pronoun being always plural in its grammar.
Likewise *you* is always plural in its grammar: *You are a good boy. You are good boys.*
But in a sentence like *You may go,* the question is that of one or more than one.

Old English made a distinction in form between the singular and plural for the second
person—corresponding to our forms *thou* and *you.* In German, Norwegian, and many
other European languages, the distinction is not so much one of singular versus plural
as it is one of formal versus informal address, *you* (Sie) being formal, and *du* being
informal. English has lost both of these types of distinction and uses *you* for all second
person occasions.

In some parts of the United States an attempt has been made to distinguish singular
and plural *you* by the use of *you* for the singular and *you-all* for the plural, but the
distinction is by no means universal: *Are you going? Are you-all going?*

indicate tense, they have, with two exceptions soon to be noted, lost the power to indicate number. *The children ran away* is no different from *The child ran away;* nor *I walk there every day* from *We walk there every day.* As regards number, therefore, it must be said that in general number is a characteristic of nouns and pronouns but not of verbs.

There are two very important exceptions to the principle I have just stated. One of them is that the verb in the present tense singular (with a noun or with *he, she* or *it* as subject) is distinguished from the plural by the addition of *-s* or *-es: The children play,* but *The child plays. The boys catch the ball,* but *The boy catches the ball.* The adding of *-s* or *-es* characterizes practically all verbs except the modal auxiliaries, which, being really past tense forms of old lost present tenses, do not come under the rule: *The children must go—The child must go. He may go—They may go.*

A second exception to the statement is to be found in the very useful but very irregular verb *be.* This verb has retained much of its old inflection and can therefore to some extent indicate number: *I am going home—We are going home. He was going home—They were going home.* Even this verb has lost the distinction of number in the second person: *You are going home* and *You were going home* have no power in themselves to tell whether one person or more than one person has been spoken to.

Thus we see that in speaking of agreement, it would be accurate to say this: *The capacity to indicate number resides in the subject.**

Person

In almost the same way the remarks about agreement in number apply in a discussion of person. Nouns have no power to indicate person and have no necessity to do so, being persons or objects or concepts spoken of. Insofar as nouns are con-

---

*Norwegian has gone even further than English. It makes no discrimination between singular and plural: *Jeg er trett* (I am tired) and *Vi er trett* (We are tired).

cerned, therefore, the statement that subject and verb agree in person is without meaning (remembering the exception I have previously pointed out of the final -s or -es on the verb).

The verb *be* still retains to some slight extent the power to indicate person: *am* and *was* for first person singular; *are* and *were* for second person singular but also plural for all three persons; *is* and *was* for third person singular. Consider the following: *I am; you are; he, she, it is. We are; they are.* And *I, he, she, it was; we, you, they were.*

As applied to pronouns, person is still a vital matter, for personal pronouns distinguish *first, second,* and *third* person: person or persons speaking—*I* and *we;* person or persons spoken to —*you;* person or thing or persons or things spoken of—*he, she, it, they.*

To conclude, the discussion of agreement of subject and verb comes down to this: that the few exceptions have acquired more significance than the statements from which they deviate. The thing to remember is that most nouns have a plural and that most verbs have a past tense.

THE MATTER OF CASE

A second common principle of grammar pertains to case. It may be briefly stated thus: Subjects and predicates are in the nominative case; complements are in the objective (or accusative) case. Again, let us see what is involved in these generalizations. As we have seen, nouns have power to distinguish number but not person. The important fact here is that neither do they have power to distinguish nominative and objective cases. Whether a noun is subject or complement cannot be determined by any case distinction within the noun itself. The question can be resolved only by word order and context. These positions are clearly defined and are in themselves sufficient to indicate their respective functions. Nouns in modern English have completely lost all distinction between nominative and objective case. There is no point in speaking of *case* in reference to them.

A distinctive form for the old dative case has also been lost.
It is now represented (a) by a prepositional phrase, usually with
to or *for: The man bought a coat for the child,* in which *child* is
the complement of the preposition; or (b) by a dative complement (usually called an *indirect object)* in a form not distin-
guishable as a case form: *The man bought the child a coat.* The
use of the indirect (or dative) complement will be discussed in
a later chapter.

Although the terms nominative, objective (or accusative),
and dative have no modern meaning as applied to nouns (we
can speak of them as fulfilling nominative, objective, and
dative functions), there is one situation in which the case of a
noun is of some importance. I refer to the use of what is called
the *independent genitive.* The old genitive case (often called
possessive) is now represented by a prepositional phrase in
ninety-five percent of its uses, nearly always with the preposition *of: The man chopped off the limb of the tree.* But in the
remaining five percent the old inflected genitive form still
lingers: *John's book is red. A fool's bolt is soon shot.* This genitive I am speaking of is an inflected genitive form, made by
adding -*'s* for the singular *(lady, lady's)* and the apostrophe
only for the plural *(ladies, ladies').* Independent genitives may
be subjects or predicates or complements: *John's is the better
horse. The car is John's. The white horse will outrun John's. It
was an idea of the Dean's.*

In discussing compound nouns I said that when two nouns
are joined in a compound—*boxcar, armchair, sunrise*—the first
noun is a modifier of the second. In such a junction the first
noun is a genitive, an old uninflected genitive, which has per-
sisted until modern times.

The modern genitive with an apostrophe and -*s* is used with
the same function as a compound noun: *a day's journey,* a genitive of extent of time; *a stone's throw,* a genitive of extent of
space; *a fool's paradise,* a genitive of description; *a boy's kite,* a
genitive of possession; *a lady's hat,* a genitive of possession or of
description, depending on the context. And we use today also a
prepositional phrase, usually with *of* as the equivalent of the old
genitive: *a piece of paper,* a genitive of material; *a piece of cake,*

a partitive genitive, the piece being only a part of the whole cake; *the song of a bird,* a genitive of description or perhaps of origin. In fact, in nearly all instances of the genitive there will be found some aspect of origin.

Case as applied to pronouns is a different matter from that of nouns. Pronouns as well as nouns may become subjects and predicates and complements, but unlike nouns they have case distinctions. Here the old rule is valid, as it is not with nouns. Subjects and predicates are in the nominative case: *I, you, he, she, it, we, they, who* are in the nominative case. Complements are in the objective case: *me, you* (indistinguishable from the nominative), *him, her* (indistinguishable from the genitive) *it* (also indistinguishable from the nominative), *us, them, whom. Which, what, this,* and *that* have lost their case distinctions. Examples: *He can go. We saw him. They will come. She saw them. Who will come? Whom did he marry? Which do you want? I want this.*

Most pronouns have genitive forms. Some of them have two genitive forms: *my, mine; thy, thine; her, hers; our, ours; their, theirs; your, yours.* The masculine pronoun has only one genitive—*his,* and *whose* is the only genitive for *who.* The independent forms are used like those of nouns—*mine, thine, yours, ours, his, hers, theirs. The hats are ours. John is a friend of mine. It* has no separate form for the independent genitive, *his* and *whose* being the only forms. The other genitive forms are used as modifiers: *my, thy, his, her, our, their, your, whose.* One still hears *mine* occasionally used as a modifier before a vowel: *Mine eyes have seen the glory.*

The forms of pronouns I have presented are the forms ordinarily used in the speech of educated persons, in which the nominative case is the accepted case for pronouns in the position of subject or predicate. It must be recognized, however, that in the speech of uneducated persons the objective case tends to prevail over the nominative even in the position of subject, to say nothing of the position of predicate. The years have brought about the elimination of case distinction in nouns except for a small percentage of genitives. It is conceivable that the distinction of cases will at some future time be eliminated for pronouns as well. The use of the objective case for pronouns used as subjects is an indication of this tendency. Strange as it may seem, the man who says *Him and me fixed the tire* may merely be a few generations ahead of his time. Recently I heard a man say this: *Us had mostly bacon and eggs for breakfast.*

An instance in which the objective case has already supplanted the nominative is that of the predicate pronoun. The form *It is me* has come into accepted use, especially in answer to the question *Who is it?* The comparable forms (*It is him. It is her. It is them.*) have not yet been generally taken up.

A curious confusion in cases is that in which a complement is put into the nominative: *John took Helen and I to the show.* This confusion of nominative for objective seldom occurs with a single rather than a compound complement: *John took me to the show, John took Helen to the show.* But *John took Helen and I to the show.* Moreover, it seldom occurs among uneducated persons, who seem naturally to prefer the objective case. It occurs in people who have been forced into some consciousness of case differences but who have not the intelligence or the industry to straighten things out for themselves. A reversal of this usage is sometimes seen in the use of a compound subject: *Him and I went to the show.*

In closing this section of the chapter, I may say that the matter of case will come up again in the chapter on verbals.

MATTERS OF TENSE

The ability of nouns to indicate number is one of the two almost universal inflections in modern English. The other is the ability of verbs, almost without exception, to indicate *present* and *past tense.* Regular verbs do so—which is why they are called regular—by adding *-ed* or *-d* or *-t* to the present form: *The man walks—The man walked. We want a dollar—We wanted a dollar. I hear the music—I heard the music. I keep my money in a bank—I kept my money in a bank.*

Certain verbs have other ways of forming the past tense.

There are some irregular verbs from Old English that have survived through the centuries. Many of them are among the commonest verbs in the language: *ride, rode; begin, began; come, came; get, got; sing, sang; swim, swam.* Three verbs—*be, go, do* —form very irregular past tenses: *was* and *were* (singular and plural for *be*), went (for go), and *did* (for *do*). A few verbs make no distinction between present and past—*cost, cut, put, shut; I cut my finger yesterday.* The auxiliary verbs are in a class by themselves. They make no distinction between present and past, for they are, as I remarked earlier, already in the past tense forms, being historically very old forms made from present-tense forms that have long since disappeared.

The development of the English language has gradually brought about the simplification of the conjugation of verbs just as it has the declension of nouns. Some verbs that were once irregular have become regular, but for the most part the Old English irregular verbs have remained irregular in modern usage. Many European languages (French, Spanish, German, for example) have many irregular verbs. These verbs, as in English, create considerable difficulty to a foreigner learning the language. Oral Swiss—there is no written Swiss language—a dialectical German, has obviated the whole problem of irregular past tenses by eliminating past tenses altogether and using the perfect forms instead: *I have gone to town* rather than *I went to town.* Children in English-speaking countries take an even easier course in that they tend to make all verbs regular: *I knowed you would bring me a present.* But we cannot in either of these ways rid ourselves of the difficult past tenses. The best we can do in the matter, as with the irregular plurals of nouns, is to consult a dictionary.

Verbs are relying more and more on adverbs to make distinctions of tense. If I say *I am going to town,* I may mean the present. If I say *I am going to town tomorrow,* I mean the future. We seldom say this: *I went to town.* Rather, we say something like this: *I went to town yesterday* or *last week* or *a month ago.* The result may be that in years to come tense forms will almost disappear, and that all verbs will attain to the sim-

plicity of the modal auxiliaries, which make no distinction as to
tense or number, though such a change is not likely to occur.

Verbs, as I pointed out earlier in this chapter, have nearly all
lost power to distinguish number: *The boy ran—The boys ran.*
An important exception to this statement, as I also pointed out,
is in the use of *-s* or *-es* in the singular present when the verb is
making a statement about some person or idea or thing. The
matter I wish to call attention to here is the fact that, if one of
the auxiliaries is used, the main verb does not change form: *The
man can walk. The boy will hit the ball. The woman must go.*
The reason for this apparently strange fact will be explained in
Chapter 11 in the discussion of the infinitive, when we shall
learn that the auxiliary was originally the main verb and that
what we call the main verb was originally a noun used as the
complement.

The inflected forms of the verb known as the *gerund* (a verbal
noun) and the two forms of the *participle* (verbal adjectives)
will also be discussed in Chapter eleven. Old English had only
two tenses—present and past—and Modern English has only
those same two tenses. What are often spoken of as *future tense*
and the *progressive* and *perfect tenses* (formed with the participles) are not inflected forms, for they are made with auxiliaries,
and so do not come within the scope of this chapter.

COMPARISON

Adjectives that express number do not vary in meaning or in
form. If a boy has four apples, he has four apples, and that is all
there is to it. If he is the fifth boy in rank, again he is the fifth
boy, and that is all there is to it. On the other hand, adjectives
that express quality may vary in degree: *One boy may be tall.
Another boy may be taller than the first. A third boy may be the
tallest of the three.* Such change to indicate degree is called
comparison. Tall is used with one *(positive degree); taller* is
used with two *(comparative); tallest* is used with more than two
(superlative). The regular endings to indicate comparison are

-er for the comparative and *-est* for the superlative. Many adjectives of one syllable use this method. Longer adjectives, particularly of three or more syllables, are likely to make their comparison in another way: by the use of *more* (notice the *r)* and *most* (notice the *s). The rose is beautiful. The second rose is more beautiful. The third rose is the most beautiful of all the roses in the garden.* Even three-syllable words sometimes use the inflected endings. De Quincey was described by Carlyle as "the beautifulest little child." The use of *more* and *most* of course is not inflectional.

Some adjectives are very irregular in their comparison: *The apple is good. The second apple is better. The third apple is the best of all.* Again: *The first apple is bad. The second is worse. The third is the worst of all.* (Notice again the *r* and the *s.)*

The comparison of adverbs is like that of adjectives. Adverbs of one syllable nearly always use *-er* and *-est—near, nearer, nearest—*whereas adverbs of more than one syllable frequently use more and most: *quickly, more quickly, most quickly.* Some adverbs, like adjectives, are irregular: *well, better, best; ill, worse, worst.* Some adverbs do not vary in form: *why, before.* With few exceptions, only uninflected adverbs become prepositions: *in, before.*

In conclusion to this chapter I remark that the details I have mentioned are about all that are left from the inflected Old English. Hundreds of years have brought the language thus far. What the future years will bring are matters only for speculation. For one thing, the invention of printing and the prevalence of dictionaries have done much to stabilize the language forms. But, nevertheless, English has become and will no doubt remain a highly analytical language, depending on context rather than on word forms for its interpretation.

ILLUSTRATIONS

Here are three true stories from the Ozark hills:

An old farmer and his wife were in a grocery store looking at

a box of avocados. The old man asked his wife, "What's them?"
To which the wife replied with an air of superiority, "Them's
avocadies."

An old Ozarks farmer was riding down the road looking for a
bull that had escaped from the pasture. He stopped to inquire of
a neighbor, "Have you seen a red cow?"—the word "bull" being
taboo in his vocabulary. "No," replied the neighbor, "but I seen
a red bull down in the woods." The farmer cried, "That's her!
That's her!" and rode away as fast as his horse could carry him.

An Ozarks Hills woman was talking to a neighbor telling how
very small she was when she was born. She was so small, she
said, that she was carried around on a pillow, and her head was
not bigger than a teacup. The neighbor in amazement asked,
"And you lived?" To which the woman replied, "They say I did
and done well."

For a change let us look at this sentence: *The oskamalagus
smurks a pingoos.* Here are three words all ending in -s. What
do you make of the sentence? Nothing, you say. You say you do
not understand it because you do not know what these meaningless words mean. Your answer is not altogether correct. For
you do have a certain amount of information. You know that
oskamalagus is the subject of the sentence, for it is preceded by
The as a signal for a noun, and it is the first noun in the sentence, where you expect the subject to be. You expect the subject to be followed by the verb. Hence you take *smurks* to be the
verb, especially since it ends in -s, the sign of the singular present. You know that whatever the *oskamalagus* is doing is going
on in the present tense. You expect the word *pingoos* to be a
complement because it follows the verb; you know the noun is
singular because it is preceded by *a,* which signals a singular
noun. Thus your knowledge comes down to your knowing that a
something is doing something to a something at the present moment. In other words, the sentence has grammatical meaning
and illustrates the great extent to which we rely on sentence
patterns for our interpretation.

8 Certain Matters of Importance

The sentences we have discussed thus far have been sentences that make statements—*declarative sentences.* The sentence order in such sentences is well defined, as we have endeavored to show throughout the discussion of the three basic sentence patterns of English sentences in Chapter four.

SENTENCE ORDER IN COMMANDS AND QUESTIONS

The word order in other kinds of sentences is not the same; it is different in *imperative* sentences and *interrogative* sentences, those that give commands and those that ask questions.

Sentences of command (and request) ordinarily have no subject. They therefore open with a verb: *Halt. Move on. Don't speak.* If the sentence has a subject, there is nothing distinctive about the word order. The subject precedes the verb: *You must move on. The soldiers must go.* The same remarks hold for sentences with incomplete verbs: *Strike the ball. The boys must go home.* And for complementary verbs: *Don't be silly.* Whether a sentence is a command or a request depends on its context and the way it is spoken.

In earlier times than ours it was customary to form a question merely by reversing the word order, so that the verb came before the subject. Such a form of question is very common in the works of Shakespeare: *Look'd he frowningly? Stay'd it long? Hold you the watch tonight?* Or to recall Sir Walter Scott's famous line: *Breathes there a man with soul so dead. . .?* But because we prefer to keep the subject in front of the verb, even in a question, we have a very effective device. We put a verb form or an interrogative word ahead of the subject as a signal that the sentence is a question, and at the same time we are able to retain the subject-before-verb sentence order that we are accustomed to in the far more frequent declarative sentences.

Questions to be answered by *yes* or *no* open with a verb form: *Must you go? Is the coat Mary's? Will it show? Has the man painted the house white? Did you find your brother well?* Often a declarative sentence is made into a question by adding an interrogative sentence modifier: *You are going to town, aren't you?*

Questions that cannot be answered by *yes* or *no* open with an interrogative:

- Interrogative pronoun as subject: *What hurt you?*
- Interrogative pronoun as predicate: *What is this?*
- Interrogative pronoun as complement: *What do you want?*
- Interrogative adverb: *Where did you get that hat? When are you going? Why can't you go?*
- Interrogative adjective: *Which car is yours? Whose hat is this?*

When the interrogative *who* is used as subject, it is in the nominative case: *Who married Ann Jones?* When the interrogative is a complement, it is in the objective case: *Whom did Herbert marry?* In informal and colloquial speech, however, this distinction is not rigorously observed. In such speech the position preceding the verb is definitely regarded as the nominative position: *Who did this?* But we find this also: *Who did he marry?* Likewise the position following the verb is regarded as the objective position, especially in response to a question: *Who is coming in?* Thus: *It's me.* These two positions of subject-nominative and complement-objective are so conventional in present usage that the case distinction of the pronoun is of decreasing importance.

APPOSITIVES

The word appositive means placed next to. An appositive is an expression placed next to another expression to help make the meaning clear. Appositives differ somewhat from modifiers. Modifiers single out some detail of meaning and attach it to the words they modify. Modifiers qualify the expressions they are attached to. Appositives do not so much qualify as explain.

Simple Appositives

An appositive is an expression by way of repetition. I may say: *I see John Jones* and then proceed to tell whom I have in mind. *John Jones is the captain of the team.* And so: *I see John Jones, the captain of the team.* I may say: *Jim saw me recently.* Well, what does *recently* mean—a month ago? last week? yesterday? To be specific: *Jim saw me recently—last week, in fact.*

Like other elements in a sentence, an appositive may be a single word or a group of words—a compound word, a phrase, or a whole sentence. Here are illustrations of simple appositives in various uses: *We went to Chicago, the largest city in Illinois. Lions are carnivorous (flesh-eating) animals. Your vote is stifling—absolutely suppressing—us. He does his work efficiently —with great skill.*

Interjections

All these uses of the appositive show a deliberate attempt on the part of the speaker to explain what he had in mind. He thought it necessary to add to his original thought the notion that Chicago, for example, is the largest city in Illinois—perhaps as the reason for his having gone there. Now there is a more primitive, though more subtle, use of the appositive than the intentional one we have been discussing.

In the very beginning of this book a dramatic scene was presented to show that meanings grow out of situations: setting, facial expression, gesture, tone of voice, and psychological reactions. And the statement was also made there that the meanings of words can never be separated from the conditions under which they were spoken. Sometimes these conditions are such as to produce unemotional speech and conversation. A man may say to me that he would like me to do an errand for him, and I reply just as casually that I shall be very glad to do his errand for him on my way to town. On many occasions, however, conversation is not so calm, and words are not so free from emotion. More often than we realize we give utterance to sounds that reveal much of what is in our mind. Suppose I ask a student to tell me what *apocalypse* means. He starts to reply, or rather he stalls in his reply: "Well, . . ." I know at once that he does not know the answer. His single word and the conditions surrounding us have been sufficient to reveal his frustration. Finally he concludes: "I don't know." I knew that fact already. His statement, "I don't know," is only an explanatory repetition of his first word, *Well*. That is, his statement is an appositive to his interjection: *Well, I don't know.* Likewise: *Ouch! I have hurt myself! Yes, I sent for you. No! You may not go!*

Interjections are often spoken of as independent words that have no grammatical connection with the sentence which follows. Such an interpretation seems to me to be without foundation. To call them independent words is to drain them of their meaning, to abstract from them the emotion which created them.

Words of Address

Words of address are closely related to interjections. Like interjections, words of address (often called *nominatives of address*—a foolish term) are usually said to be independent words. But again, like interjections, words of address do have a grammatical connection with the sentences which contain them. Given a speech situation between two people, with its attendant circumstance, the direct address will be found to contain within itself the meaning which the sentence states more explicitly. Suppose Charles is playing in the back yard. His mother calls him: "Charles!" Charles, pretending ignorance, calls back: "What do you want?" He knows perfectly well what she wants. She calls: "Come here!" Her call is only a repetition of his name as she spoke it in the first place. *Charles* and *Come here* have identical meanings, and the boy and his mother are both aware of this equivalence. Two more examples: *Mary, do not hurt the little kitten! John, you are lying to me.*

Sentence Appositives

There is still another aspect to the subject of appositives. This is the use of one sentence as an appositive to another sentence. It grows out of the fact that there is in the first sentence some word, like a pronoun, that looks forward to and demands an explanation of the thought contained in the first sentence. This use, though not common in formal writing, is frequent in conversation. It is a very ancient manner of speaking, going back hundreds of years; its continuance through the centuries proves its usefulness and vitality.

Let us take this sentence: *He is a good boy, your son is.* The pronoun *he* is left unexplained until the second sentence tells who *he* is. For the reason that the pronoun points forward to an explanation it is called a *determinative.* (We shall meet this word many times again. It means seeking an end; it is the same word that is to be seen in *terminal,* the place where a bus route, for example, comes to an end.) The pronoun *he* seeks an end— an explanation. The closeness of the two sentences is further to be seen in the fact that *is* in the second sentence is left high and dry without a predicate, its predicate *(good boy)* being carried over from the first sentence. We often omit the second verb altogether: *She is a good cook, my wife.* This sentence pattern is

frequently used in Spanish, so frequently indeed as to be almost
the most common of Spanish patterns: *Es de Los Estados Unidos mi esposa* (She is from the United States, my wife). We use
this appositional form in questions: *What do you mean, you
can't go? What are you saying, no money? Isn't it foolhardy, the
trip to New York?* Likewise in Spanish: *?Es de Los Estados
Unidos su esposa?* (Is she from the United States, your wife?)

In these sentences, as in the case of the appositives already
discussed, we have an explanation by way of repetition in order
to make a statement or a question clear. The result is not two
sentences; it is not a compound sentence made up of two
mutually self-sufficient clauses. It is one sentence made up of
two interdependent sentences, the second repeating and explaining the thought contained in the first.

The matter of appositives in some such form as this will be
very essential to an understanding of certain sentence patterns
to be discussed later when we come to the complex sentence.

IT AND THERE AS SUBJECTS

We need now to discuss two closely related sentence forms.
These are the sentences that begin with *it* and *there*. Let us take
it first.

It as Subject

Students who are familiar with the Latin language will recall
that while Latin verbs may have nouns as subjects—*Puer
puellam amat* (The boy loves the girl)—no personal pronoun,
on the other hand, is essential as a subject. Thus *Amo te* means
I love you, and *Amabat canem* means that *Someone—he, she, it
—loved the dog.* Verbs like *amo,* however, do have a subject. A
person or thing is the subject about whom or which something
is said, a subject being implied in the inflection of the verb. A
similar condition exists in English in our verbs of command and
request. When we say *Go away,* we imply the presence of a person who receives the command. The verb *go away* contains the
subject within itself.

The point here is that there are certain verbs in Latin which do not even imply a subject, verbs like *pluit,* which means that *rain is falling.* These are called *impersonal verbs,* because no person or thing or other subject can in any way be identified as doing anything. The verb contains in its single self the capacity to make a statement. In modern English we have no such subjectless verbs, and so we have no way to translate a Latin verb like *pluit.* We do not say *Rains.* The best we can do is this: *It is raining.*

In the early stages of our language there existed such subjectless verbs: *Then happened there came in to me heavenly Wisdom.* In this case *happened* has no subject. Why, then, do we not simply say *Snows* or *Rains,* instead of the longer forms: *It is snowing* or *It is raining?*

We have previously spoken—especially in Chapter six—of the development of a sentence order in the elements that make up a modern English sentence. The development was, as we have seen, partly the cause of the dropping of the old inflectional endings and partly the result of that loss. At any rate, the effect of a clearly established word order was that at last there was no place for subjectless impersonal verbs. And thus the old subjectless impersonal verbs passed out of existence. The neuter pronoun *it* came into use as this needless subject. *It* has little meaning; the word satisfies our demand for a subject. The sentence did not need a subject, but we gave it one just the same. *It* does not state what is raining—merely that *it* is raining. Examples: *It seems to me. It is no use. It was a long time ago. It must be two hours after sunrise.*

Another use of *it* as subject is closely related to *it* as the subject of an impersonal verb. Let us examine a sentence: *It is hard work, that job of yours.* Such a sentence is much like the one we discussed a little while ago—the sentence appositive. The subject here has more meaning than in the impersonal sentence. Here in this sentence the subject points forward to an explanation of what the speaker has in mind. *It* here is determinative. Sometimes *it* is called an *anticipatory subject,* which is not a bad name in that the indefinite subject does actually announce that a specific meaning follows in the second sentence. Examples: *It is getting so you can't buy much for a dollar. It used to be very hard for me, the way my father made me work.*

There as Subject

We come now to *there* as subject. This word, too, is sometimes—though wrongly, I think—called an independent word, an expletive, serving to introduce the real but delayed subject. I cannot agree with such an interpretation. Let us examine a sentence: *There are two men in the room.* As I understand the sentence, we are not talking about *two men.* We are not saying this: *Two men are in the room.* Rather, *two men in the room* is our assertion; the conditions at the moment are such that two men are present in the room. Just as we use *it* to represent the general but undetermined conditions implied in the impersonal verb—*It is raining*—so in the sentence under consideration we use *there* to represent the general situation about which the predicate is made: *are two men in the room. There,* like *it,* is an indefinite but real subject, and the predicate noun *men* performs, as all predicate nouns do, the function of making the statement the speaker wishes to convey.

The interpretation I have presented has precedent in Old English usage. Note the following: *Thaer sceal beon gedrync and plega* (There shall be [must be] drinking and play [merriment]). The word *thaer* is followed by a singular verb *sceal; gedrync and plega* constitute the predicate after the complementary verb *sceal.* As in modern English the verb is sometimes in the plural: *Thaer waeron sume of thaem bocerum sittende and on hiera heortum thencende* (There were some of the scribes sitting and in their hearts thinking). The subject *thaer* is in this sentence followed by a plural verb, *waeron,* and a pronoun, *sume,* referring to a plural, *scribes.* This variableness in the number of the verb after *there* has sometimes been argued against the interpretation of *there* as subject. But this variableness occurs also in modern English: *There was a man in our town. There were two men in the room.* The objection is further obviated by our use of variable number in other constructions: *What is this? What are these? Which of you is going? Which of you are going?*

We have another use of *there* that we must not overlook—

namely, its use with a complete verb: *There came a terrible storm. There once lived a very wicked king.* What shall we say of sentences like these in which no predicate noun occurs to bear the weight of the assertion?

I believe the answer to this question lies, as we have already pointed out, in our decided liking for nouns and adjectives as predicates, in our habit of throwing on such words the weight of making a statement more emphatic than the verb itself is capable of making. As before, *there* is a nominal subject—indefinite, to be sure—pointing forward to more specific and definite explanation of what is in the speaker's mind.

There once lived—something, someone—it is not stated *what* or *who*. But something or someone once lived. What was it? Who was it? It was a *king*. This is another manifestation of our tendency to make predicates out of nouns and adjectives. *King* is not the delayed subject of *lived* but the predicate noun of an appositional sentence, appositive to the subject *There lived*, and thus a predicate noun gaining the added emphasis desired by the speaker—a most useful device thoroughly in accord with other English practices. Examples: *That night there came a storm. Suddenly there walked in two men with masked faces.*

The matter will come up again in Chapter eleven in the discussion of the so-called independent participle and infinitive. For this reason the discussion here may not be quite so much ado about nothing as it may have seemed.

COMPOUND ELEMENTS

Any of the sentence elements we have studied may be compounded. In themselves compound elements offer no particular problems. Here are numerous illustrations:

- Compound subject: *Men, women, and children go to the movies.*
- Compound predicate verbs: *The man went to town and bought a hat.*
- Compound complements: *I bought a hat and a coat.*
- Compound discontinuous verbs: *The work made me tired and cross.*

- Compound appositional adjectives or nouns: *I found the child ill and feverish. I thought the man a scholar and a gentleman.*
- Compound predicate adjectives or nouns: *The man looks tired and ill. The man is a gentleman and a scholar.*
- Compound adjective modifiers: *The strange but pleasant music charmed me.*
- Compound adverb modifiers: *The boy walked slowly and carefully down the street.*
- Compound prepositional phrases: *I went to the drugstore and to the meat market.*
- Compound complements of a preposition: *The car could not move through the snow and ice.*
- Compound appositives: *My daughters, Mary and Ann, bought some flowers.*
- Correlative conjunctions: *I own both horses and mules. The boy was neither bad nor dull. The man played the game not only slowly but also carefully.*

Here is a little mystery story full of compound elements:

The day was singularly dark and dreary. The clouds hung low over hill and dale. I was riding through the woods and through the fields. My horse picked his way slowly and carefully over the rocks and across the streams. At nightfall I came upon a tumbledown and deserted cottage. The sight of its broken windows and of its sagging doors made me very sad and disconsolate. Unexpectedly a man came from behind the house and spoke to me very quietly. I had not seen him before that moment. Without a minute's warning he lifted a rifle and pointed it straight at me.

You may imagine the proper ending and finish the story for yourself. Then you will be satisfied.

ILLUSTRATIONS

There was once a little girl. She lived with her mother in a little house. They were very poor and did not have much food. One day the mother sent the little girl to the woods.

"Child, perhaps you can find some wild berries. Won't you bring some berries? I am very hungry."

It was a pleasant day in summer. The girl wandered into the woods and finally met an old woman. The old woman spoke to her.

"Why are you out in the woods?"

"I am hungry. I am hunting for wild berries."

The old woman pulled out a little iron pot from under her cloak.

"Look, this is a magic pot. It will cook food for you. You must speak to the little pot. 'Little pot, cook for me.' You must speak to it again. 'Little pot, stop.'"

The little girl thanked the old woman and ran home. This was a nice present for her mother. The little girl and her mother would never be hungry again. The pot would always fill up with porridge.

One day the little girl was away from home. The mother got hungry and wanted some porridge. The pot filled with porridge at her word of command.

The mother could not stop the pot. She did not know the right words. Porridge came from the pot in a stream. It ran over the stove and spread over the floor. It ran out of the door and trickled down the street.

Soon the porridge reached a house at the edge of the village. The little girl was visiting in that house. She saw porridge everywhere. She ran home through the streets. She went into the house and into the kitchen.

"Little pot, stop."

The pot stopped instantly. The people of the village ate porridge for three weeks.

What is the moral of this little story?

One morning in winter, long ago, an old black crow sat on the branch of a tree. In his beak he held a delicious bit of cheese. The crow was, of course, very happy about his piece of cheese. It would make a fine breakfast. At any rate, he thought so.

Presently a fox came along and smelled the cheese. He went and stood under the tree. He spoke very politely to the crow.

"Good morning," he said. "You are looking very well today."

The crow was happy. Naturally, he could not say anything. His mouth was full of cheese.

The fox spoke again. "You have very beautiful eyes and very beautiful feathers."

Still the crow could say nothing. He sat in the tree and swelled with pride.

The fox spoke again. "You must be a beautiful singer, surely." Then the crow opened his mouth and cawed loudly. The cheese dropped right into the fox's mouth!

"Thank you very much," said the fox.

The fox was happy. "Another time, perhaps, you will not sing! You are a very poor singer. You should not listen, next time, to foolish words."

With a wave of his tail the fox trotted off into the woods.

9   Compound Sentences

We have studied the fundamental patterns as they appear in the simple sentence. We have now to take up the combination of two or more of these sentences into somewhat more complicated sentences. Such combinations of sentences result in compound and complex sentences.

The difference between compound and complex sentences is said to depend on the way the simple sentences are put together. If simple sentences are so combined as to be thought equal in importance, the sentence is called a *compound sentence.* If the sentences are so combined as to make one of them seem to be the important element, with one or more others dependent on it, the sentence is called a *complex sentence.* The distinction between compound and complex sentences, however, is more apparent than real.

The most primitive kind of compound sentence is that used by children and by grown people who are not scrupulous in casting their statements into careful form. Such a sentence is merely one statement after another joined by *and:* "We went to town and we went to a grocery store and we bought some candy and Johnnie ate too much candy and he got sick and I didn't eat too much candy and I didn't get sick and Johnnie had to have the doctor and the doctor gave Johnnie some medicine and then Johnnie got well again," and so on, almost in one breath. "And

English Education Resource Center
University of Wisconsin La Crosse

then I says to Jim, I says . . . and Jim says to me . . . and Mary says to Jim . . ."—pause for breath—"and Mary then . . . and I says . . ."

Sentences like these are the common stock of conversation. What we call complex sentences have arisen out of just such masses of sentence material. Complex sentences are refinements of compound sentences. They are the result of a realization that the relations between the parts of a compound sentence can be more clearly defined and that finer shades of meaning can be expressed by making one clause more important than the rest. It is no wonder, then, that no sharp line of distinction can be drawn between compound and complex sentences. Complex sentences are only compound sentences more explicitly stated.

The complex sentence is more exact than the compound sentence. But in many ways the compound sentence is more rapid than the complex sentence. The common people have something to be said for their clearly marked preference for the compound sentence. What the complex sentence gains in exactness it sometimes loses in vividness and speed. Extemporaneous talk and informal writing will make much use of the compound sentence, and rightly so. More careful speaking and writing will use an intermingling of complex sentences, and again rightly so.

Although the distinction between compound and complex stentences is not sharp—nor the distinction between coordinating and subordinating conjunctions—we shall present these two kinds of sentences one at a time. Because compound sentences are more elemental we shall take them first.

Coordinating conjunctions join the clauses of compound sentences. Though they are rather extensive in number, they are not extensive in meaning. The conjunction most frequently in use is the one expressing the notion of addition, one statement added to another of similar nature and purpose. This conjunction is *and: I went to town and there I bought a hat.* Sometimes a compound sentence expresses contrast, with *but: I went but Mary stayed at home.* A compound sentence may present a choice of possibilities, with *or: James must study harder or he will fail.* A coordinating conjunction is sometimes used to explain what the speaker had in mind as his reason for saying what he said in his first clause: *It will rain soon for the barometer is falling.* (The sentence does not say the barometer's falling is the cause of the rain, but the statement is presented as evidence on which the prediction of rain rests.)

Coordinating conjunctions are of two kinds—those we have just been illustrating, called *simple conjunctions,* which do nothing but join clauses without doing much to express anything like accurate relationships; and those which, in addition to joining clauses, are adverbs as well, and as a consequence make relationships more precise than the simple conjunctions can make them. Conjunctions of the second type are called *adverbial conjunctions.*

An adverbial conjunction is the equivalent of a simple conjunction plus an adverbial phrase. *Likewise,* for instance, means *and in the same way; then* means *and after that; however* means *but on the other hand.* We can illustrate only a few of the numerous adverbial conjunctions: *He was stupid; moreover, he was bad. I thought him a coward; however, I could trust him for this task. I had no money; so I could not go to the show.*

It often happens that two or more clauses are put into one sentence without the use of a conjunction. Such sentences are survivals of the ancient practice of putting sentences together and of leaving the hearer to make his own connection: *I went to town; Mary went to school. The asparagus has been nice this year, we have had a great deal of rain.*

While we are on the subject of compound sentences perhaps we should speak of the *comma splice* (which in former times failed many a freshman theme). There are two kinds of sentences in which no conjunction is expressed. These should be kept distinct in our minds. To use a comma as a careless substitute for a period or at least a semicolon is of course unjustifiable. As a matter of fact, joining two clauses together is often unjustifiable. It all depends on the sentence. Consider this: *I am going to the show now, I bought a pound of nails.*

Such a sentence would tax one's comprehension under any circumstances. Unless there is something in the context to show why these statements are related, the clauses should hardly be written together. It would take more than appears on the surface to justify even writing the one after the other.

The other kind of "comma splice" is quite a different matter. Consider: *The asparagus has been nice this year, we've had a great deal of rain.* To object to a comma splice here is to ignore the ancient sentence pattern by which two sentences were placed next to each other. For example, this Old English sentence in close translation: *He you in swimming beat, had more strength.* Here the relation is obviously one of cause: he beat you *because* he was stronger. In the sentence we are discussing we have the same relation: *cause.* The asparagus has been good *because* there has been much rain. Hence *The asparagus has been good, we've had a great deal of rain* is a good sentence, justified by present-day usage, as anyone can quickly discover for himself.

ILLUSTRATIONS

Once upon a time there were three Billy Goats. They were named Gruff, and they lived on the side of a mountain. On the mountainside there was very little food, but across the valley was a beautiful pasture of green grass. On the way to the pasture there was a bridge; it crossed a small stream. Under the bridge lived an ugly, old troll.

One fine day the youngest Billy Goat Gruff started across the bridge.

"Who trips over my bridge?" the troll roared loudly.

The littlest Billy Goat Gruff answered in a very soft voice. "I am the littlest Billy Gruff."

The troll came out from under the bridge. "I shall eat you at once."

"Don't eat me. My bigger brother is coming after me. Why not eat him?"

The troll grumbled but he said nothing more, and the littlest

Billy Gruff went on his way to the pasture.

Presently the next Billy Gruff came over the bridge. Again the troll came from under the bridge.

"Who trips over my bridge?" Again the troll roared and grumbled, but he did not eat the Billy Goat Gruff. He would wait for the biggest Billy Goat Gruff.

Soon the biggest Billy Goat Gruff came over the bridge; he stopped right in the middle of the bridge. He was not afraid of the wicked troll; so he stood there and waited. He was very strong; moreover, he was a brave goat.

"Who tramps over my bridge?" The troll roared very loudly at the Billy Goat Gruff, but the Billy Goat did not move.

"I am the biggest Billy Goat Gruff; I tramp over your bridge. Can you stop me?"

"I shall eat you at once; you will make a good dinner for me."

Up came the troll. The Billy Goat put his head down and pushed the troll off the bridge into the water.

After that the troll was never seen again. The three goats went to the pasture every day and got very sleek and fat.

Now, that's the end of the story. Would you have been afraid of the troll or would you have stayed on your own side of the bridge?

10   Complex Sentences

Complex sentences may contain noun clauses, adjective clauses, or adverb clauses. The facts (1) that all three kinds of clauses are used as single parts of speech within one of the simple sentence patterns, and (2) that all three are, as we shall see, really appositive sentences and hence practically alike in origin and use, are a sufficient justification for presenting them together in one chapter.

NOUN CLAUSES

Many noun clauses are introduced by *that,* a fact which needs some explanation. The word goes back to the time when two sentences were merely put together, and the reader had to make his own association. *That* was originally a determinative (We have met the word *determinative* before, as meaning a word that looks forward for an explanation.) used as the subject or the predicate or the complement in the first of these sentences, and the other sentence was a sentence appositive to explain what was meant by *that: That is true: the world is round.* The second sentence tells what it is that is true. Hence, from its position in front of the clause, we developed *that* as an intro-

ductory word of a noun clause, just as we developed prepositions out of adverbs placed in front of nouns: *That—the world
is round—is true. That—there had been a mistake—seemed
certain.*

The noun clause used as complement is another illustration
of how *that* came to be used as it is. Take the sentence *He said
that he could come.* What did he say? He could come. In *He
said that—he could come,* the second clause explains the determinative *that: He said that he could come. He doubts that
the train will be on time.* Here is an Old English sentence in
literal translation: "He saw that Apollonius so sadly sat and all
things beheld and no thing not ate." These remarks are true
also of a predicate clause after a complementary verb: *The
truth is that:* What? *He will never come.* Examples: *The truth
is that he will never come. His statement was that he would
come tomorrow.*

There are still other uses of noun clauses:

- As complement of a noun: *He had no proof that Jane was still
alive.*
- As complement of an adjective: *He felt certain that she would
return.*
- As appositive: *The fact that you are coming comforts me.*
- As subject of an appositive: *It is unfortunate that he should
fail.* Sentences like this one in which a clause is used as the
subject of an appositional sentence are in very common use
today: *It is most unlike you that you do not comprehend this
matter.*
- The noun clause introduced by *that* seems not to be used as
the complement of a preposition, though such usage was common in Middle and Elizabethan English. The following sentence was written about 1585: *Your thoughts are ridiculous,
for that things immortal are not subject to affections.* In
modern usage *for that* would become the subordinating conjunction *because* (a fact that shows how closely noun clauses
and adverbial clauses are related, as we shall see when we

study adverbial clauses). A similar instance is the old use of *till* (until) with *that* as its complement and a clause appositive to *that: From the time he was very small till that he was grown* (Fra thaet he wass full litell till that he waxenn wass).

Numerous as are the noun clauses introduced by *that*, many noun clauses are not so introduced. Indefinite, relative, and interrogative pronouns, adjectives, and adverbs are also used and occasionally an exclamatory adjective or adverb.

- Indefinite pronoun: *What he does is no concern of mine.*
- Indefinite relative adjective: *You may take whichever road you like.*
- Indefinite adverb: *The woman did not know when the boy came home.*
- Exclamatory adjective: *What a soldier he became was a cause for wonder.*
- Exclamatory adverb: *How foolish he was always amazed me.*
- Still other words: *I cannot say whether I shall buy the coat. James does not know if he can go. His reason was because he did not have the car.*

Purists will rule out *because* and *if* as introducing a noun clause on the ground that they are subordinating conjunctions introducing adverb clauses. It is safe to say that such an objection cannot be upheld in current usage, as a few minutes' reading or listening to the speech of cultivated persons will reveal. On the other hand, many persons still prefer to say, "The reason is that. . . ."

Sometimes, frequently in fact, noun clauses are not introduced by any word at all: *He said he would not go. I am sure you are right.* Sentences introduced by no word whatsoever are not to be thought of as sentences from which the introductory word has been dropped. They are simply survivals (or perhaps revivals) of the old language custom of placing two sentences side by side and letting the hearer establish the relationship for himself.

Perhaps we should illustrate direct quotations: *The man*

said, *"I cannot sell the house." "I cannot sell the house,"* said the man. *"I cannot,"* said the man, *"sell the house."*

Before we leave the matter of noun clauses we should call attention to the similarity between sentences with noun clauses and those we talked about in the chapter on simple sentence patterns: *The man thought me a liar.* With a noun clause the sentence reads like this: *The man thought I was a liar.* The introduction of a verb before *liar* has changed the form of the pronoun from *me* to *I.* The difference is partly one of emphasis but only partly so. *Me* is the complement of *thought* as well as the subject of *liar,* where *I* is the subject of *was a liar* and the whole clause is the complement of *thought. Thought* does not have quite the same meaning in the two sentences.

The matter is clear enough in sentences like these. But some confusion arises in complex sentences which contain a clause like *I think: He is a man who I think will do you good service.* Even though *who* is the subject of *will do,* it is so closely related to the verb *think* that it is rather naturally attracted to *think* and regarded as a complement: *He is a man whom I think will do you good service.*

In such sentences there is a strong tendency to use the objective case, a tendency which has considerable justification. Anyone who analyzes himself in the process of saying such a sentence will discover that he feels the pronoun first as the complement of *think* and only second as the subject of its verb, *will do.* A careful observer will be conscious that he must make a mental adjustment to prevent his saying *whom* before he puts the pronoun into the nominative case, which its use supposedly demands. It is an instance of psychology against the so-called logic of grammar. That is why many persons other than grammarians talk this way: *He is a man whom I think will do you good service.* In fact, this very sentence I have been discussing came to me from the dean of the College of Liberal Arts in one of our largest universities. But the day has not yet come when *whom* is acceptable to persons who pride themselves on the purity of their speech, though the celebrated late Professor Jespersen used to uphold the idiom.

ADJECTIVE CLAUSES

Adjective clauses have the same origin as noun clauses—the placing of two simple sentences together: *John is driving the car. He bought it yesterday.* One who hears or reads these two sentences together finds in them more connection than the mere fact that one follows the other. He pushes the meaning to make a relation between the car John is driving and the car he bought yesterday, and realizes that the car being driven today is the same car that was bought the day before. The word *the* is a determinative; it points ahead to an explanatory appositive: *John is driving the car—He bought it yesterday.* Or we may say this: *The car—John is driving it—He bought it yesterday,* or *John is driving the car he bought yesterday.*

The dropping of the personal pronoun from the second sentence was an ancient way of showing that the second clause was closely related to the first and subordinate to it: *John is driving the car he bought* (it) *yesterday,* or *The car John is driving* (it) *he bought yesterday.* This method of subordination by omission of the personal pronoun is much used in modern English: *He is the man I am looking for. The book you want is in the bookcase.*

Contrary to the impression some people have about them, such sentences have not dropped the relative pronoun *(who, which, that, as).* They are properly to be regarded as survivals (or rather revivals, for there was a time in the eighteenth century when omitting relative pronouns was altogether out of fashion) of the old sentence appositives we have spoken of so frequently.

The verbs in these adjective clauses are left standing alone, for the old pronoun has been dropped as the sign of subordination. Even a complementary verb is left without a predicate pronoun: *I am not the man I was.* Curiously enough, if the omitted personal pronoun was a subject, a relative pronoun is nearly always used in the adjective clause: *The man* (he) *who came is a doctor. I saw the man* (he) *who sold the car.*

If, as we have seen, one sentence can be made subordinate to another by dropping the personal pronoun, how does it happen that we have complex sentences with relative pronouns? The answer lies in the fact that, in addition to the personal pronoun in the second clause, an indefinite pronoun (not properly a relative pronoun) like *that* was also frequently used, just to make assurance doubly sure: *John is driving the car—that one—He bought it yesterday.* Such a sentence has two determinatives, *the* and *that*. (I am inclined to believe that *the* is always a determinative, referring ahead to some specific thing: *We saw the parade.* What parade? The parade known to the hearer.) Both *the* and *that* point forward to an explanation: *John is driving the car—that one—He bought it yesterday.* In German there is a similar use: *Er ist der Mann der hat das Geld gebracht* (He is the man—the one—that brought the money). In such a sentence there is no real relative pronoun; the second *der,* as well as the first *der,* is a determinative.

In time the word *that,* or whatever indefinite pronoun was used as a determinative, became a relative pronoun looking backward to an antecedent instead of a determinative pointing ahead to an appositive sentence: *John is driving the car—that—he bought it yesterday* drops the personal pronoun *it* and becomes *John is driving the car that he bought yesterday,* with a relative pronoun of which *car* is the antecedent.

That the transformation of determinative into relative pronoun is not always complete can be seen in these two genuine sentences from the Ozark Mountains: *He is the man the weevils et* (an old past tense of *eat) his berry patch. The heifer had a bell on which it might of got tore off.* These are interesting folk speech. In the first sentence the word *the* points ahead to identify the man to be spoken about; the personal pronoun *his* has not been made into a relative *whose* nor has it been dropped. As it stands, ungrammatical as it is, it is far more picturesque than its "grammatical" equivalent: *He is the man whose berry patch was eaten by weevils.* The second sentence has some interesting features also. *Of* is a common mispronunciation of *have,* the auxiliary; and *tore* is the past tense used for the perfect participle, *torn.* But the significant feature is that while the sentence has developed the relative pronoun *which,* it has not dropped the personal pronoun *it.*

The most common relative pronouns in addition to *that* are

who, which, and *as,* all of them used in the same way as *that: The girl who wears the red sweater is a sophomore. We sold the car to a Mr. Smith whom we had known. You may take such books as you will need. (As* is the complement of *will need; such* is a determinative looking to the clause for explanation.) *Mary met the man to whose house I went.*

In present usage we sometimes try to distinguish two kinds of adjective clauses, those which are called restrictive clauses and those which are called nonrestrictive clauses. A restrictive clause is often used to tell which one out of many objects or persons of its class the speaker had in mind. There are, for example, many men who are sent to prison. Which one is meant when one hears that *the man* was sent to prison? He can be identified. He robbed the bank. *The man who robbed the bank was sent to prison.*

On the other hand, some clauses refer to places or things or persons the identity of which is already known to the hearer. He knows *what* or *whom* is meant as soon as he hears the word. He can identify Chicago without any further information. *We went to Chicago, which is one hundred miles from home.* The name of Chicago is recognized and would be whether the distance to it is mentioned or not.

Difficulty often arises in the attempt to distinguish these two types (if they really are types), for strictly speaking only adjective clauses which modify proper nouns (or their equivalents, like *my father*—there being only one) can be truly nonrestrictive clauses. And so the puzzling over the matter of names is not a very justifiable expenditure of energy.

It is only since the eighteenth century that *who* has been used exclusively to refer to persons and *which* to antecedents other than persons. Hence the old form of the prayer: *"Our Father, which are in heaven." That,* as now used, refers to both persons and things.

ADVERB CLAUSES

In the beginning of the chapter on compound sentences I remarked that the difference between compound and complex sentences is more apparent than real, the question being one of the relative importance of the sentence elements. Before I take up the matter of adverb clauses I wish to present three sentences for discussion, one from Old English and two from our contemporary usage. Here is the old sentence (in translation): *He his life saved and he was often wounded.* It is obvious to any present-day reader that *and* is not an additive conjunction. *And* here does not mean *more of the same.* The sentence means that he saved his life *although* he was often wounded. In form the sentence is a compound sentence; in meaning it is a complex sentence. The important fact is that *he saved his life* in spite of the less important fact that *he was often wounded.* It is a complex sentence of concession—an *although* sentence.

My other sentences are these: *Do that again and I'll whip you;* and *Feed a cold and starve a fever,* a bit of advice all too often misunderstood and mistakenly followed. In these two sentences *and* again does not mean *and* as we ordinarily define *and. And* here clearly means *if: If* you do that again I'll whip you; and *If* you feed yourself when you have a cold, you will later have to starve yourself when you have a fever that will follow. Again the two sentences are compound in form but complex in meaning. They are adverbial complex sentences of *condition, if* sentences.

Adverb clauses have the same origin as noun and adjective clauses, namely in a sentence appositive and its preceding sentence, with a determinative pointing ahead to an explanation. And we find here the same process at work by which determinatives were transformed into connectives. We have explained the old sentence: From the time he was very small till that he was grown, in which the expression *till that* emerged as a subordinating conjunction. *Till that* (till what?) *he was grown.* That is to say, from the time he was small *until he was grown*— a complex sentence. Just as relative pronouns emerged from determinatives and indefinite pronouns to create adjective clauses out of sentence appositives, so subordinating conjunctions emerged out of determinatives and indefinite adverbs to create adverb clauses out of these same sentence appositives.

Let us take the word *where* for an example. The original ad-

verb was *thaer. He lay there—he fell.* Where was *there?* It was
the spot where *he fell. He fell* is an appositive to explain where
there was. Here is an interesting old sentence from about the
year 1000: *Thaer thin gold is thaer is thin heorte.* (There thy
gold is, there is thy heart.) The first *there* points forward to the
second half of the sentence; the second *there* looks back to the
first half of the sentence. These two *there's* would later fuse into
one subordinate conjunction. In time the old indefinite *hwaer*
took the place of *thaer* and merged into the second clause as
where. He lay—where—he fell. Thy heart is where thy gold is.
Occurring as it did before the appositive clause, *where* became
associated with the clause as a conjunction rather than with the
preceding clause as a determinative. This transfer of association, like that occurring in adjective clauses, explains what I
mean when I say that in reality all clauses—noun, adjective,
and adverb—are noun clauses.

We can illustrate only a few of the numerous subordinating
conjunctions and their uses: *I shall come when you want me.
After I have gone away, you will be sorry. I would go were I not
otherwise engaged. (Were* serves both as a connective between
the clauses and as a complementary verb in the adverb clause,
which means this: *If I were not otherwise engaged*—a condition
contrary to fact. I *am* otherwise engaged and so I cannot go.)
More examples: *Stubborn though he was, he often heeded advice. Whichever road you take, you will have a detour. I shall
come as soon as I can.* A conjunction like *as soon as* is complex,
for the word *as* has an interesting origin. It has been made from
two old words that have been fused together. Take this expression: *Swa micle swa.* It means *as much as,* for *swa* means
so. Now let us join *swa* with *eall,* which means all. Thus *eall swa*
means *wholly thus.* Now, pronounce *eall swa* very rapidly and
you will end up with *also,* which again means *wholly thus.* Now,
pronounce *also* very rapidly and you will end up with *as.* Hence
as means *wholly thus.* Hence *as soon as* means: *I shall come
completely soon.* How soon is that? *As I can.* The second *as* is
the complement of the old auxiliary verb *can* and an appositive
to the first *as,* which modifies *soon.* Examples: *I shall come as*

soon as I can. He was as busy as he could be. Go just as you are.
In the last two sentences *as* is both conjunction of manner and
predicate pronoun.

Here are two interesting sentences: *The more, the merrier.
The more he has, the more he wants.* Notice that the *the* in these
sentences is not the *the* we know as the definite article, as in *the
horse.* In these sentences *the* is a very old word, which was once
the instrumental case of *that.* The word in such sentences therefore means *to the extent. By how much he has more, to that
extent he wants more. To the extent that there are more people
present, to that extent is it the merrier. The* is therefore an adverb in these sentences.

No enumeration of the uses of adverb clauses can be made.
One reason is that the functions of adverb clauses overlap and
fuse into one another, so that it is often difficult or even impossible to tell which function is intended. Only by hearing the
sentence spoken in actual discourse can one tell what the
sentence really says. Another reason is that, as in the case of
prepositional phrases, there are as many functions as there are
conjunctions—a situation further complicated by the fact that
many prepositions and conjunctions have more than one meaning according to how they appear in one context or another.

One more matter. Certain adverb clauses present an interesting grammatical problem which is the center of considerable
discussion. These are clauses, particularly, which point out an
exception or which make a comparison. An illustration of the
former is the famous line from Shakespeare's *Julius Caesar:* "I
do entreat you, not a man depart, *save I alone,* till Antony have
spoke." And for the second, here is a short sentence: "John is
taller than James." In this respect the sentences are alike—
both *I* and *James* have no verb.

The consequence of this omission is that the conjunction is
gradually being thought of as a preposition and the clause as a
prepositional phrase. What were subjects are being regarded as
complements of prepositions: *The whole class assembled except
John,* or *There is no one in the house but me.* In such sentences
but, except, and *save* have pretty well passed back to their orig-

inal function as prepositions, with nouns and pronouns—the latter in the objective case—as their complements. What about *than* and *as?*

Let us take these sentences: *He is as tall as I am. He is taller than I am.* If we omit the verb, as we did with *but, save,* and *except,* we have these: *He is as tall as I. He is taller than I.* Now what shall we do? Shall we continue to insist that *I* is the subject of a suppressed verb? Or shall we use *me,* and say that *me* is the complement of *than* and *as? He is as tall as me. He is taller than me.* It is altogether likely that popular speech will in time answer the question for us, or rather, that it is in process of answering it right now; and that verbless clauses with a subject will come to be regarded as prepositional phrases with a complement.

VERB CLAUSES

We have seen clauses functioning as nouns, adjectives, and adverbs. A question remains: Do clauses function also as verbs? I am inclined to the opinion that they do, in at least one kind of sentence that is common in conversational English. This is a sentence with what on superficial view merely looks like a repeated subject. But there is still to be determined what lies under this very frequent use of the repeated subject so characteristic of folk speech.

Let us look at one of these sentences: *My wife, she is a fine cook.* One explanation is that *she* is an appositive either as essential to identifying her or as giving additional information about her. But I cannot see that *My wife, she is a fine cook* is like either of these: *My brother James went to town,* or *Chicago, the largest city in Illinois, is on Lake Michigan.* Here *James* and *city* are clearly appositives.

Nor is the sentence like the sentence appositives we have already discussed: *She is a fine cook, my wife.* Here we have a statement repeated in an appositive form to tell who *she* is, where *she* is a determinative pointing to *wife* as an explanation. But in the sentence under consideration there is no call for further information, for the words *my wife* furnish all the identification needed.

I propose that *my wife* is the subject of the sentence—the person about whom some statement is to be made. What is said about her? That *she is a fine cook.* Hence I interpret the assertion as a verb clause of which *my wife* is the subject. I would give a similar interpretation to the words of a famous hymn: *The prince of darkness grim—we tremble not for him. Prince* is the subject, and *we tremble not* is the verb clause predicate.

ILLUSTRATIONS

A long time ago there was a boy who watched the sheep. Every day he took the sheep to a pasture on the hillside, and there he sat and watched them all day long. In the evening, when the sun went down, he drove the sheep home again.

He often became very lonely because he had no playmate. He wanted company during the long hours of the day.

One day, when he was very lonely, he remembered what his father had told him when he first took charge of the sheep.

"You must always be on the watch for the wolf," said his father. "If you see a wolf, you must call for help as loudly as you can."

The boy had never seen a wolf, and so he was not afraid of one. All he could think of was that he was very lonely. He decided that he would call "Wolf!" at the top of his lungs.

The people in the village heard his call. They dropped their work, seized their axes, and ran up to the pasture where the boy was. When they got there they saw only the boy and the sheep.

The men forgave the boy for the bad joke, but they told him that he must not do such a thing again.

One day he was feeling lonelier than ever. He knew that he should not call, but he called out just the same.

Again the men came up the hillside. Again they found only the boy and the sheep. This time the men were very angry. They told the boy that he must not deceive them again.

One day, as he was watching the sheep, he saw a big gray wolf. It came out of the forest. The boy called as loudly as he could.

The men in the village heard his cries. They thought the boy was only fooling them again, so they did not go up the hill.

The men finally thought about the matter and decided that they had better look into it. Perhaps there was a wolf, after all. They went up the hill as fast as they could run.

They were too late. By the time they got to the place, the wolf had gone back into the forest. All that the men found was the boy's hat. The wolf had eaten the boy and the sheep.

Is not this a sad story? How would you like a situation like that of the little boy? Would you have called "Wolf"?

11   Verbals

We have spoken many times of the resourcefulness and flexibility of the English language in bending its materials to suit its needs. We have seen its inventiveness in the development of prepositional phrases, in the subordination of clauses, in the free transfer of one part of speech to another. Among the evidences of this adaptability nothing is more striking than the usefulness of the verbals.

There are three verbals in English: the gerund, the infinitive, and the participle.

THE GERUND

A gerund is a noun. The word comes from a Latin word which means *to carry, to perform.* Gerunds are not the only nouns of action in English; they are only more expressive of action than some other nouns. Strictly speaking, by tradition, the gerund is a verbal noun ending in *-ing,* as *running, talking, swimming.* Let us look at the gerund *arriving,* and we can thus show that the word *gerund* need not be limited to nouns ending in *-ing.*

Suppose we start with a conventional sentence: *When the Duke arrived, he caused great stir.* Here *the Duke* is the subject of the verb *arrived.* We may restate the sentence in a somewhat similar way by making the meaning of *arrived* (verb of action) into a noun of action: *The Duke's arrival caused great stir.* The verb in the adverb clause has now become a noun, and the verb in the main clause has become the verb after *arrival,* but (the important fact) *the Duke* is still the subject of *arrival.* The Duke was the person who acted, the person who arrived.

That many such nouns contain verbal meaning is of course clear from the fact that they may take a complement or have adverb modifiers. See Shakespeare's line *".. . to suppress his further gait herein,"* in which both *further* and *herein* are adverbs modifying the noun *gait.* Again: *The Duke's arrival the next day caused great stir,* in which *the next day* is the *when* complement of *arrival.*

Why the subject of these verbal nouns is in the genitive case is an interesting point in the history of our language. We must recall what was said earlier about compound nouns and the development of prepositions, to the effect that compound nouns had their origin in the extremely ancient Indo-European custom of placing one noun (in an uninflected genitive case) in front of another to show relationship between them: *sunset, tomato can, weather forecast.* Gradually, except where the compound nouns survived, the old uninflected genitive was removed from its position in front of the noun it governed and was placed after its noun in the form of a prepositional phrase: *the pages of the book, the roar of the wind, the day of judgment.*

In the meantime there had developed an inflected genitive form (at first only in the masculine genitive) which ended in *-es* and which later changed from *-es* to the apostrophe and *s* (*'s*) as we have it today. Thus an expression like *John book* became *John's book,* and *the Duke arrival* became *the Duke's arrival* or *the arrival of the Duke.* All this amounts to saying that when a noun is brought into relation with another noun, it is in the genitive, as (1) a compound noun or (2) an inflected form in *'s* or (3) a prepositional phrase.

We have not space here to present the many uses of the genitive, but we can point out three or four. We are all familiar with the possessive genitive, so much so that many persons think the genitive means only possession: *John's hat.* But there are many other important uses as well: genitive of material, as *sandpile* or *heap of stones;* descriptive genitive, as *a man's hat;* genitive of extent, *an hour's delay;* appositive genitive, *the office of mayor;* and so on.

Of these uses the two that concern us here are those called subjective and objective genitives. If we think of *sunset* we are conscious that the sun is doing something, performing the act of setting. Hence *sun* is the subject of *set;* and *the roar of the wind,* wherein *of the wind* is the subject of *roar;* it is the wind that is roaring. Parallel to the subject genitive is the objective genitive: *woman hater,* where the woman does not hate; she is hated by someone. Or *the clerk's dismissal,* where clerk is the object—the person who was dismissed. A similar situation exists in *money getter.*

The traditional gerund differs from a noun of action as we ordinarily think of it chiefly in the fact that the gerund with its ending in *-ing* contains more of the content of a verb. *The Duke's arriving* is more expressive of action than *the Duke's arrival.* In fact, the gerund as we conceive it today has more verbal content than it originally had. We make more distinction between *arriving* and *arrival* than would have been made in, say, the year 1000. Being of the nature of a verb, it takes a subject: *the Duke's arriving* or *the arriving of the Duke;* and it may take an object: *the destroying of the city.*

The verbal noun has many uses:

• As subject: *John's knowing where the trouble lies helps us.*
• As predicate noun: *His business was answering letters. His* is the subject of *business; answering* has no subject for its subject is carried over from *business.* The person who does the business is the person who is *answering* letters. *His* is the subject of both verbal nouns. Historically *letters* is an old uninflected genitive; *answering of letters,* an objective genitive.

When the order is reversed and the verbal noun becomes the subject, followed by a complementary verb and predicate noun, the verbal noun has to supply its own subject: *Running is good exercise.* Which is to say this: *Anyone's running is good exercise for that person.*

The following is another example in which the gerund has to supply its own subject: *There was no living with him after that. There was no* (not anyone's) *living with him after that.*

- As subject of a sentence appositive: *It was a disappointment, not seeing you again.*
- As object complement: *I resented your coming. I dislike working in a garden.* These two illustrations of complements show the difference spoken of. *Your* is the subject of *coming,* inasmuch as you and I are different persons, and so the subject cannot carry over from *resent* to *coming. Working,* on the other hand, needs no separate subject because *I* who *dislike* would be the person to do the *working* in the garden.
- As complement of a preposition: *He could not come on account of Jane's being away. I have the task of running the lawn mower.* In the second sentence we have an appositive genitive: *running the lawn mower* is what the *task* is.
- As an element in a discontinuous verb: *I got the pump to working.*
- As complement of an adjective: *I was not conscious of his disliking me. He said he did not feel like going home.*
- As complement of a noun: *I had no knowledge of his coming. I had an idea of her thinking that she was not welcome in her son-in-law's house.*

The subject of the verbal noun, as we have seen, often takes the form of a propositional phrase. But the transformation of the old genitive into a phrase does not alter the fact that the verbal noun still has a subject. Examples: *The arrival of the Duke caused great stir,* where the phrase *of the Duke* is the subject of *arrival;* or *The rushing of water made much noise,* where *of water* is the subject of *rushing.* The same condition prevails with the objective genitive, in which a noun serves as the complement of another noun. *The clerk's dismissal was inevitable,* or *The dismissal of the clerk was inevitable.* The objective genitive in some ways resembles the subject of a passive

verb (to be discussed later in this chapter) in that the identification of the person doing the act is often of no great
importance: *The clerk was dismissed. The dismissal was inevitable.*

We have talked much of the genitive subject of the gerund.
The genitive, however, is not always used. Some words have no
genitive form: *He would not agree to that being true,* in which
case *that* has no genitive. Groups of words are not easily put
into a genitive form. *You would not be surprised at one so poor
as I needing help. What did he say about you and me going
together?*

Again, there is in the use of the genitive the same tendency of
the objective case to prevail over the other cases that may be
found in other instances. The use of the objective is not limited
to the speech of the unlearned, but is to be found among good
writers as well. *We laughed at the thought of you going. Who
would ever imagine him doing that? I had no idea of John going
home.*

THE INFINITIVE

The infinitive, like the gerund, is a noun, and its meaning,
like that of the gerund, has become considerably stronger with
the passing of time. The infinitive was once inflected like a
noun. There were two forms (the old genitive having disappeared long before). One was a form used in the nominative-
accusative case, which has been preserved as our *simple infinitive* (without *to*); the other was a form derived from the old
dative case, which has been preserved, as many old dative
forms have, with *to,* as our *prepositional infinitive.*

The *simple infinitive* at that time was limited almost wholly
to its use as the complement after incomplete verbs. This
means, in modern times, that the simple infinitive is limited
almost wholly to its use with auxiliary verbs. We must understand that what we call auxiliary verbs were originally incomplete verbs with meanings of their own and that they

required complements, a function which the infinitive as a verbal noun could very well fulfill.

After the Norman Conquest auxiliaries came more and more into use. Certain old incomplete verbs (like *can, must, should*) gradually lost their meaning and developed into helping verbs which became exceedingly useful in the expression of many kinds of statements. Just as the forms of the verb *be* (which was originally a complete verb) became useful with predicate nouns and adjectives, so these old incomplete verbs as auxiliaries became useful in many ways.

As the auxiliaries lost their meaning they came to rely more and more on the infinitives which were serving as their complements, with the result that the infinitive, which had hitherto been a complement, was absorbed into the verb and actually became the important element in the verb phrase. As a consequence of the transformation of these old incomplete verbs into auxiliaries, we are able to convey a great variety of meanings we could not otherwise convey: *I may sing—I must sing—I should sing,* and so on. Especially useful is the formation of the so-called future tense, made with the infinitive and the auxiliaries *shall* and *will.* These auxiliaries, like all other auxiliaries, had meanings. *Will,* for example, meant an expression of intention to do some act: *I will go* or *I intend going.* That is, the expression is in the present tense referring to an intended act to be performed at some later time. Likewise *shall* meant to be under an obligation. *I shall go* meant that *I am under an obligation to go* at some later time. Inasmuch as the act referred to some later time, *will* and *shall* were fused with the verb: *will go* and *shall go.*

In combination with an auxiliary verb, the simple infinitive is no longer felt as a complement, any more than the auxiliary is distinctly felt as a meaningful verb. At the same time I think it may be doubted that these auxiliary verbs ever lose their content entirely or that the simple infinitives with an auxiliary ever cease entirely to function as complements. At least one adds life to these old verbs if one can still perceive in them some of their old original incompleteness and their need of a complement.

In Shakespeare's *Hamlet* is an interesting passage in which the verb *can* is used both as a main verb and as an auxiliary. The proximity of the two uses is significant as showing that the transformation of a main verb into an auxiliary had not been completed by the year 1600. *"Try what repentance can what can it not? Yet what can it when one can not repent?"* The first three uses of *can* show it as a main verb, an incomplete verb with *what* as its complement. The last *can* is an auxiliary with the infinitive *repent* made into the main verb.

We take now *the prepositional infinitive.* The prepositional infinitive with *to* was derived from the old dative case, which was governed by the preposition *to.* Eventually the dative ending was dropped, and the infinitive was left with *to* as its preposition. This infinitive (unlike the one in the accusative case) was a prepositional phrase modifying the verb (as other prepositional phrases were in the beginning). *To* meant *toward, in the direction of.*

I am going to town meant *I am going in the direction of town* (expecting to get there). *The man is going to die* meant that the man is going in the direction of death. *He had an ambition to become rich* meant that he had an ambition directed toward riches. In modern times the preposition *to* has almost wholly lost its meaning of direction and is felt to be merely a part of the infinitive—a fact that has some bearing on the problem of the split infinitive, as we shall see.

The infinitive with *to* was closely related to a verb of motion and was a modifier of the verb: *I went to buy a hat.* Before *to* lost its force as a preposition, it would have had *buy* as its complement. Subsequently the preposition and the infinitive were fused into a unit and were not thought of as preposition and complement. Once the unit was created, it could, like the prepositional phrase, be moved to other positions in the sentence.

- As subject: *To buy an expensive overcoat seems foolish.*
- As subject of a sentence appositive: *It is not necessary to go.* The use of the infinitive in such sentences is of very great importance.

- As predicate noun: *Our purpose has been to help you.*
- As complement: *I do not pretend to say what you should do.*
- As one of two complements: *He promised me to go.* That is, it was *he,* not *I,* that was to go.
- As complement of a noun: *He made no attempt to pass the examination.*
- As retained complement after a passive verb: *He was said to be afraid.*
- As complement of an adjective: *I am afraid to go.*
- As complement of a preposition: *Our grocer is about to retire from business.* (*About* is the only preposition used in this way.)
- As modifier of a verb: *He saved his money to buy a watch.*
- As modifier of a noun: *The way to do this is to buy your materials first. I have only a minute to stay.*
- In combination with various verb forms to make verb phrases: *You ought to buy a hat. I am not able to buy a hat. I ought not to have to buy a hat. I shall have to go home.*

The infinitive may be combined with the same indefinite relative pronouns, adverbs, and adjectives as are used with noun clauses: *What to do was the question. We don't know where to go. She knows nothing but how to sweep a room.* The infinitive is used after subordinate conjunctions (which might better be called prepositions in this instance): *You can't do better than to buy the house. I had rather be shot than to go there now. I was mad enough to cry.* (Perhaps the infinitive here is really appositive to *enough.*)

Two other uses may be mentioned here:

- As sentence modifier: *To tell you the truth, the man is a fool.*
- As an exclamation: *Oh, to be in England, now that April's there!* (Browning)

We have yet a very important use to discuss. This is the so-called "infinitive with subject accusative." The matter is by no means so complicated as has sometimes been made out. We need primarily to recall two of our simple sentence patterns from Chapter four for the infinitive with subject accusative is only another manifestation of these two ways of making sentences. We remember that an incomplete verb often absorbs an adverb: *The boy held the book up.* We remember also that such a verb may absorb an adjective or a noun or a pronoun: *The man painted the fence white. The exercise made me tired.* Now the infinitive we are here presenting has the same pattern: *The man made the car go.* Here *car* is the complement of *made-go.* There is nothing new in the construction, except to point out that the "subject accusative" in such a sentence is actually a complement and not a subject at all. As before, the verb has absorbed the infinitive as part of itself to make a discontinuous verb.

Now for the second sentence pattern. We remember this sentence: *The man found the child ill.* And we remember that *child* is the complement of *found* and the subject of *ill.* This sentence pattern leads us to the infinitive with a real subject accusative, for here the complement of the verb is also the subject of the infinitive. The two sentences are alike: *The man found the child ill. The man wanted me to go.* In other words: *The man found that the child was ill. The man wanted that I should go.* There is this distinction in the two sentences: The infinitive, being a verbal and hence expressive of action, has a genuine subject, whereas *ill,* being an adjective, is a predicate adjective and must be indicated as such.

Here is an interesting sentence dated January 2, 1567, in which Queen Elizabeth reportedly said, "I may not suffer you to depart without that mine admonition may show you harms and cause you shun unseen peril." The first infinitive, *to depart,* is a prepositional infinitive with a subject *you.* The second infinitive is in the old simple infinitive construction—*shun* as the infinitive with *you* as its subject. The distinction between simple and prepositional infinitives was evidently not clear in Elizabethan England, for here is a portion of another sentence from the same date as the above: "Which what they be, time may teach you know."

The infinitive with a subject is intimately related to the infinitive introduced by *for: I am hoping for you to go.* Such an expression has an interesting origin. The infinitive was in the beginning the complement of *am hoping,* and *for you* was an old dative phrase modifying the verb: *I am hoping for you that you can go.* We have seen in numerous other instances that a sentence element becomes detached from its original element and attaches itself to the element following it. Out of such a process prepositions, subordinating conjunctions, and relative pronouns arose. Just so, the phrase *for you* left its verb and attached itself to the infinitive. The old complement of the preposition has become the subject of the infinitive.

The *for* infinitive is very useful in sentences with *it* or *there* as subject: *It is not wise for you to go. There is no need for you to go.* Once formed as a unit, the infinitive with *for,* like the prepositional phrase, was capable of being moved about in the sentence—as subject for example: *For you to go would be unwise.* It may also become the subject of a passive verb: *For you to go is thought to be unwise.* In contrast, the infinitive without *for* cannot be used in these ways. We do not say such things as these: *Him to go was made possible. Car to start was got by me.* The infinitive with *for* took over its subject from the old dative (now indistinguishable from the objective), and so when a pronoun is used it is in the objective case: *For us to do what you ask is impossible.*

The infinitive with *for* and a subject should not be confused with another form now almost gone out of use in educated speech, which is a preposition *for* followed directly by an infinitive rather than by a noun or a pronoun. The most familiar example is a Negro spiritual: "Swing low, sweet chariot, coming *for to carry me home."* This infinitive, however, is still much used in folk speech: *"I'm just fixin' for to go to town."*

Before we conclude with the infinitive we should speak briefly of the *split infinitive,* over which considerable discussion has raged. Much depends upon the interpretation of the *to* which precedes the infinitive. Originally *to* was a preposition, and the infinitive, a verbal noun, was its complement. When *to* lost its meaning as a preposition of direction, it became a sign for the infinitive itself to distinguish it from other forms of the verb. As long as *to* was regarded as a preposition, no adverb intervened between *to* and the infinitive, for the preposition and the infinitive were felt to be a unit in themselves. The modifying adverb therefore preceded the phrase: *I came merely to ask a question.* When *to* ceased to be a preposition, however, and became only an introductory sign, then all that followed *to* could be regarded as a unit, and an adverb modifier would no longer be an intruder between the preposition and its complement: *He tried to so conduct himself as to make his position sure.* It cannot be denied that in many instances the split infinitive is a distinct aid to clear expression. It is, no doubt, a construction which will eventually place itself squarely within the pale of accepted usage, however much debate it may be subjected to by the would-be learned.

THE PARTICIPLE

The participle, in constrast to the gerund and the infinitive, which are verbal nouns, is a verbal adjective. Originally its form for the present tense was distinct from that of the gerund, for it ended in *-ende, -inde, -ynde,* or *-ande,* whereas the gerund frequently ended originally in *-ung.* Since the disappearance of the gerund in *-ung* in the thirteenth century, the similarity in form between the present participle and the gerund in *-ing* has been a source of some confusion. In spite of the fact that both gerunds and present participles now end in *-ing,* the two are essentially different in meaning.

The participle has many uses in modern English. In fact, the frequency and adaptability of the participle constitute an interesting characteristic of present-day English. In its present and past tenses it meets many needs, particularly in the formation of predicates and as substitutes for adjective and adverbial clauses. In these uses, the adverbial use especially, it has a swiftness of movement that the clause cannot attain, for it need not bother about being too precise in stating relationships.

I shall present first some of the simpler uses and then pass to more complicated matters:

- As a vivid modifier of a noun: *The girl's glancing eyes surveyed the room.*
- As a noun: *The living inherit the problems of the dead.*
- As an adverb: *The iron is scorching hot.*
- As predicate adjective: *The child sat there dangling her legs from the chair. The village lay sleeping in the moonlight. The old man sat buried in thought. I read the book sitting up in bed.*
- As appositional predicate: *I found him lying on the floor. I could feel myself being strangled.*
- As an element in a discontinuous verb: *The conversation got him badly worked up. I had the book read by midnight.*
- As adjective following its noun: *The old man sitting by the fire longed for peace. He is a man enslaved by ambition to become rich.*

Now for the use of the participle in the formation of verbs:

Passive Voice

When we were discussing complements in the chapter on the basic sentence patterns, we pointed out that object complements differ from other complements in that they can be turned around to become the subject of a sentence: *The boy threw the ball* can be this: *The ball was thrown by the boy. The boss fired the clerk* becomes this: *The clerk was fired by the boss.* Not only has the complement become the subject, but the verb has changed as well. We have inserted a form of the verb *be* before the verb. And we have changed the verb from a past tense to a past participle.* (Regular verbs have the same form for past

---

*I do not mean to say that only past tense verbs can become passive verbs. *The boy throws the ball. The ball is thrown*—these sentences are in the present tense. The point is that the passive voice requires a past participle.

tense and for the past participle; but the functions are different. The past participle, it must be remembered, is an adjective.) Such a change in the verb is called the *passive voice,* in which the subject of the sentence instead of performing the action (as in the *active voice*) is acted upon. The *ball* did nothing; the *clerk* did nothing. What was originally the subject has become the complement of a preposition. In a sentence in which it is not important to tell by whom the action was performed the phrase is dropped: *The ball was thrown. The clerk was fired.* This remark is especially true in sentences like these: *The fence was painted white. The boy was named John. Was the fence painted white?* The adjective or noun which was previously a part of the discontinuous verb has become a predicate adjective or noun after a passive verb. Only incomplete verbs with object complements have passive voice. The reason is obvious. A complete verb has no complement that can be turned into a subject, and complementary verbs do not express action.

Infinitives as well as main verbs can have passive voice: *The boss was obliged to fire the clerk.* That is, *The clerk had to be fired.* It is a curious fact that sometimes an infinitive has an active form but a passive meaning. Note this German sentence: *Hunde sind an der Leine zu führen*—Dogs are on the leash to lead. That is, dogs are *to be led* on the leash. We have a similar use in English: *Room to rent,* or *House to let.* The room is to *be rented;* the house is to *be let.*

We sometimes convey a passive meaning without the use of a passive verb. An illustration may be found in the first sentence of Chapter seven in this book: "The discussion thus far has limited itself to the basic structures. . . ." Here is a different way of saying the same thing: *"The discussion thus far has been limited. . . ."* This method of using a reflexive pronoun instead of a passive voice is very common in Spanish: *El sol se pone*—the sun puts itself; the sun sets. *Se habla italiano*—Italian is spoken here; Italian speaks itself.

Indirect and Retained Complements

The retained complement arises from the use of a passive

verb. It arises also from the use of an indirect complement. For that reason I shall discuss the indirect complement first.

We have just said that only incomplete verbs can have a passive voice. Another remark applies to them also: Only incomplete verbs with objects can have an indirect (or dative) complement. In some instances it is not enough to know what action was performed; we want to know to whom or for whom it was performed.

In Old English this indirect complement was in the old dative case, a case which has disappeared from our language or rather which has fused with the old accusative (objective) case. In the structure of a sentence, the indirect complement precedes the object complement: *John gave the man a dollar.* The man is the indirect complement; *a dollar* is the object complement.

Like the genitive case, which uses the alternate form of a prepositional phrase instead of the inflected genitive ending in the apostrophe and -*s*, the dative, or indirect, object is often expressed in the form of a prepositional phrase, usually with *to* or *for*: *Will you give the money to the boy? Will you do this for me?* In its prepositional form the dative phrase differs from the dative (indirect) complement in that it is not limited to use with incomplete verbs. It may be used with complete and complementary verbs: *John will come for me. The car belongs to me. He was kind to me. This seems silly to me. She was a good wife to me. The dress was too long for her. It looked like a fortune to me.*

While modern English has no case that can be called dative as distinct in form from the nominative-objective form, the feeling for the old dative still persists even with complete and complementary verbs. A youngster six years old traveling with his parents, who were a little uneasy as to whether a hotel reservation would be kept for them, asked anxiously, "Will there be *us* a room at the hotel?" Hundreds of old datives occur in the works of Shakespeare, none more clear than when Petruchio bids his servant knock at the gate: "Knock me here soundly . . . Knock me at this gate and rap me well, or I'll knock your knave's pate."

Now the *retained complement.* The discussion here is based

on the two immediately preceding: that of the passive voice and that of the indirect object. The point about the passive voice is that the object may be turned into a subject, and the active verb turned into a passive verb. The point about the indirect object is that the verb in such a case has two complements, a direct object and an indirect object, with the indirect object preceding the direct object. Usually the *what* or *whom* complement becomes the subject. But it sometimes happens that the indirect object rather than the direct object is converted into the subject of a passive verb. Out of a sentence like *I gave the man a dollar* we may have the regular passive voice: *A dollar was given to the man.* Suppose we reverse the order and use the indirect object for the subject: *The man was given a dollar.* Thus we keep the object in its original position after the verb. In such a sentence *a dollar* is the retained complement—retained in its position after the verb.

The participle is used in the *formation of verbs:*

Progressive forms represent action as continuing. The participle, like the gerund and the infinitive, has gained through the centuries more verbal meaning than it originally had. What we now call the progressive forms of the verb are made out of the present participle plus some form of the verb *be,* often with the help of an auxiliary verb: *I am going,* or *I must be going.* We think of *going* as part of the verb phrase. Historically it is not a part of the verb. *Must* was a notional incomplete verb with *be* as its infinite complement and *going* as an attribute predicate. But the fusion of the three words results in a verb phrase—*must be going*—where *going* has lost all of its adjectival quality.

An interesting example of the early stage before the participle became part of the verb phrase may be seen in the old medieval play of *Abraham and Isaac,* in which Isaac asks his father to explain his absence to his mother by telling her this: *I am in a far country dwelling.* In this case, *dwelling* is still a verbal adjective. Modern English would have fused the words into a verb phrase: *I am dwelling in a far country.*

Perfect forms, actually a past tense, represent action as completed. Let us take this sentence—*I have the work finished*—in which *finished* is clearly an adjective describing the condition of the work: The work is finished. Or again: *I have a chicken killed and dressed.* This is to say, I have a chicken in the condition of having been killed and dressed. These two words describe the chicken. They are adjectives, verbal adjectives. Now let us move the verbal adjectives next to the verb: *I have finished the work. I have killed and dressed a chicken.* Have has ceased to be an incomplete verb and has become an auxiliary. The old participle has become the main part of the verb and is no longer regarded as an adjective. This use of a form of *has* plus a past participle makes up what is now known as the *perfect tense.*

Sentences with the so-called perfect tense may be cast into progressive forms: *I have seen the show—I have been seeing the show. John had played ball—John had been playing ball.* And they may be used as questions: *Have you played ball?—Have you been playing ball?*

I come now to the use of the participle as a *sentence modifier.* The participle frequently functions as an adverb clause used as a modifier of a sentence. Let us take the sentence familiar to all who once knew the old Reed and Kellogg grammar (which still influences me, I confess): *Hearing a step, I turned.* The grammar—quite erroneously, I think—makes *hearing* a modifier of *I,* following the definition of a participle as a verbal adjective. But surely the sentence does not mean this: *I, who heard a step, turned.* No, the participle has here the force of an adverb clause. That such is the case, of course, cannot be determined except by context, and it sometimes cannot be determined even then. If it had been necessary to state the meaning definitely, the speaker would have used a clause with a carefully chosen subordinating conjunction in place of the participle. So what does *Hearing a step, I turned* mean? Was it *when* I heard a step, *after* I heard a step, *because* I heard a step, that I turned? The answer is that it makes no difference: *Having done the chores, I went into the house.* This use of the participle is sometimes hard to distinguish from that of its use as predicate adjective: *Smiling sweetly, the girl turned away. I hid quickly, hoping that the man would go away.*

A use of the participle grammatically similar to that of sentence modifier, but illogical in content, is the *dangling participle.* The trouble with the dangling participle is that the subject of the participle is not the same as the subject of the verb. In the sentence *Hearing a step, I turned,* the person who heard the step was the person who turned. And it was *I* who hid quickly, and *I* who hoped the man would go away. If we introduce a subject for the verb that is different from the subject of the participle, we are likely to produce a most ludicrous effect: *Coming down the street, a large house is seen.* Obviously, the house is not coming down the street. One needs only to get rid of the passive voice, and thus give the verb and the participle the same subject: *Coming down the street, the man saw a large house.* Remember one thing: *Get rid of the passive verb!*

There are occasions when this use of the participle does not disturb the reader because he is so slight a degree conscious of the difference in subjects that the illogicality of the sentence is unnoticed: *Beginning in September, the fee will be one hundred dollars.* I doubt that the reader feels the force of the participle at all (in which case, I suppose, it isn't really a participle), for he is conscious primarily of the time and extent of the change—and so the fact that *fee* and *beginning in September* have no logical relationship does not disturb him. Such a participle, however, must be used with caution and with skill.

As we have had occasion to say many times, the English language is a most versatile language. We have here another illustration of this versatility. The participle which is a sentence modifier, we have seen, has much the effect of a clause, but with more directness and less accuracy of expression. Sometimes we desire to have both the directness and the accuracy (like eating one's cake and having it too). As a consequence, we often introduce the participle with a subordinating conjunction: *While crossing the street, I fell down. I stopped at Mary's when going to town.*

We come now to a use of the participle which some people refuse to accept on the ground that it is a dangling participle, but which has come into such general use that it is mere pedantry to deny its propriety. It is not a dangling participle at all. It may be called a *consequential participle,* because the meaning conveyed by the participle follows as a consequence of the action expressed by the verb: *He came early, causing me much annoyance,* or (with a conjunction) *He came early, thus causing me much annoyance.* Those who object to this construction do so on the ground that there is no word for the participle to modify, whereas the truth is that the participle is not a modifier at all. It is, rather, an equivalent to the second part of a compound sentence. Moreover, there is no illogicality because the verb and the participle have the same subject.

I take up now a construction which partly has to do with the participle and partly not. Like the consequential participle it has been the subject of considerable mistaken discussion. I refer to what is called the *nominative absolute.* The name hasn't much meaning, except as an occasional pronoun may find its way into the construction, for nouns make no distinction of cases except for the five per cent of inflected genitives which still survive. The characteristics of the nominative absolute are (1) that it contains a noun or pronoun followed by various words or combinations of words as an appositional predicate related to the noun or pronoun; and (2) that there is seemingly no word in the sentence which the absolute can be attached to. But the nominative absolute is not so mysterious as it sounds.

The nominative absolute is a survival of an ancient dative form that was used by way of imitation of the ablative absolute in Latin. In the beginning both the Latin absolute and the English dative were adverbial clauses in which a noun was the subject, and the participle or an adjective or a second noun was the predicate. Inasmuch as many ancient clauses, as we have already seen, had no complementary verb in them, such a joining of subject and predicate without a verb was no unusual phenomenon, being merely an appositional sentence used as an adverb.

The fact of subordination was indicated in Latin by the ablative case, in Old English by the dative. When in the course of time the English inflections disappeared and no distinction was made between dative and nominative forms, the construction was mistakenly called the "nominative absolute." For many years the objective case was sometimes used for pronouns as being nearer the old dative form and is heard even yet on occasions: *I don't expect much, him being what he is.* But for the most part a pronoun as the subject of an absolute construction, like the subject of a verb, is in the nominative case.

The nominative absolute is sometimes called an independent element: *The sun having set, I went home.* Such an interpretation is unsound both historically and logically. Historically, the construction is a modifier of the verb. Logically, it bears a relation to the sentence, however much that relation may lack of being clearly stated. There is no reason, therefore, why the nominative absolute should not be put in its proper place as an adverbial sentence modifier: *I went home, my work being done.*

Though the absolute construction most frequently makes use of a participle as its predicate, there are other forms as well:

- Two nouns: *Myself a guest in the house, I did not feel like interfering in the domestic quarrel.*
- Noun and adverb: *Supper over, we went back to the sitting room.*
- Noun and infinitive: *I send you ten dollars now, the rest to come soon.*
- Noun and prepositional phrase: *He sat there, his feet on the table. John was reading, his eyes on his book. I am going ahead, your advice to the contrary.*
- Reverse order: *Granted the chance to go, the trip would be impossible.*

Before we leave the participle perhaps we should speak of a very common colloquial expression that looks like a participle. Take a sentence like this: *I should like to go to New York, being as I have never been there.* Or this: *I think I shall buy a new coat, seeing as how the old one is worn out. Being* and *seeing* probably once functioned as participles; now they are in such uses nothing but conjunctions.

ILLUSTRATIONS

There was once a poor woodcutter who had to work very hard to get enough food for himself and his wife.

One day when he was about to cut down a tree, he heard a voice speaking to him.

"Please do not cut down my tree."

The woodcutter was very much surprised and stopped to look about him. He saw a strange-looking little man dressed in green.

"I beg of you, do not cut down my tree. This is where I live. If you cut down my tree, I shall have nowhere to go."

The woodcutter promised not to cut down the little man's tree.

Then the little man in green told the woodcutter that by way of payment for his kindness he could have three wishes granted. The woodcutter rushed home to tell his wife about the good fortune that had come to him.

"Now we can have everything we want! We can have a nice cottage to live in and a cow and some chickens."

The woodcutter's wife was disgusted with him. "If we can have anything we want, why do we not ask for a castle? Then I can be a queen. We shall have a golden castle. We can't get anything without asking for it."

The woodcutter wanted a cottage to live in. He and his wife argued all day about whether to ask for a cottage or to ask for a castle. Finally they realized that they were hungry, for they had not eaten anything all day.

"I am hungry," said the woodcutter. "I wish I had a piece of sausage."

There, in front of his face was the most beautiful sausage you ever saw.

"Idiot!" exclaimed his wife. "You have used up one of your three wishes."

"I wish the sausage was on the end of your nose," said the woodcutter, becoming very angry.

There, sure enough, the sausage was on the end of the wife's nose!

"Now your second wish is gone!" she cried in rage. "Why don't you wish for the castle we talked about? I should look fine with a sausage on the end of my nose!" And the poor wife broke down and cried bitterly.

The woodsman did not know what to do. Finally he said very solemnly, "I wish the sausage was off the end of my wife's nose."

Instantly the sausage disappeared, and the woodcutter and his wife never saw it again.

They sat in their little cottage in silence. They had had their three wishes granted, but they had profited them nothing.

12   Punctuation

Since the early twentieth century many teachers of composition have believed that punctuation serves one purpose only, to show the structure of a sentence. In keeping with their concept they have for years frustrated their students and themselves in a vain attempt to make of punctuation a system of automatic rules.

Such persons have overlooked the original and even more important purpose of punctuation—the essential purpose of all punctuation—to show how a sentence was intended to be read. Insofar as sentence structure is an aid to understanding a sentence, all well and good. But comprehension of a sentence is more immediate and direct than comprehension of its structure. Knowledge of structure is more likely to follow than to precede comprehension of sentence meaning. The reader does not become aware of the structure of a sentence until he has become aware of its meaning.

The rhetorical function of punctuation (that is, its aid in reading or speaking) has been lost in favor of the more limited function of showing structure. This loss is much to be regretted, for rhetorical punctuation can be made an instrument of great flexibility and resourcefulness in conveying sentence meanings, which, occurring as they do on a cold page of printed paper, need all the help they can get.

Fortunately present-day composition is in a state of reaction against stereotyped processes and is freeing itself from many of the restrictions imposed on it by the tyrannical taskmasters of the past generation. Many marks of punctuation formerly thought necessary to fulfill some structural requirement are now omitted, and many marks not needed to show structure are now thought to be desirable.

In spoken discourse the beginnings and endings of sentences are usually made clear by the tones in which the first and last words are uttered. Facial expressions, gestures, postures—the whole physical aspect of communication—convey not merely the meanings of words but structure and punctuation of sentences as well. In written discourse the eye, which sees words rather than hears them, needs aid just as the ear needs it in oral discourse. Punctuation constitutes this aid.

TERMINAL PUNCTUATION

As a matter of custom a sentence opens with a capital letter as a visual aid to mark its beginning; the capital means nothing except as it makes for ease in reading.

As a matter of custom also, for ease in reading and for clearness of meaning, a sentence ends with one or another of three terminal marks of punctuation. Of these the *period* is by far the most frequent, being used to end statements of all kinds: *Birds fly. They went home. The man became ill. The boys have gone. I have no money. A cord was stretched across the room from one side to the other. No one could believe the story.*

Next in importance is the question (interrogation) mark: *Who is coming? Whom did you want? Will you do this for me? Where are you going? What do you think he will do? Don't you ever think of what this means to me? What are you doing that for?* An interrogative sentence ordinarily opens with an auxiliary verb or with an interrogative of some kind. Many declarative sentences, however, may be made into questions by using a question mark instead of a period: *The man became ill? They went home?* Such sentences indicate a certain degree of surprise or other emotion and are usually a repetition of the declarative sentence that preceded them in the discourse.

Sentences like the last two are closely related to sentences of exclamation, which express a considerable degree of emotion. Declarative and interrogative sentences may be made into exclamatory sentences by the use of an exclamation mark:

The man became ill.　　　The man became ill?
They went home.　　　　They went home?
You are teasing me.　　　Are you teasing me?
The man became ill!
They went home!
Are you teasing me!

These remarks also apply to sentences of command: *Do not come. Do not come? Do not come!*

INTERNAL PUNCTUATION IN SIMPLE SENTENCES

The basic simple sentences are closely knit units. As such they require no internal punctuation so long as they move straight ahead in their natural sentence order. They require internal punctuation only when some element is added to them either by way of an interruption inside them or by way of an introduction or an afterthought. Such added elements, while valuable to the meaning of the sentence, are not closely enough related to the basic sentence to be regarded as an integral part of it. In this way they differ from modifiers that are vital to the communication of the intended meaning. The insertion or the omission of commas as internal marks of punctuation can, therefore, be an efficient means of showing delicate shades of meaning within the writer's mind.

Consider this: *Nothing, however unimportant, can be omitted. However unimportant* interrupts the flow of meaning: *Nothing can be omitted.* Again: *An old man, terrible in appear-*

ance, knocked at the door. Old is an adjective related to *man,* whereas *terrible in appearance* is additional but not basically essential material. This distinction pretty generally applies to objectives which follow rather than precede their nouns. The distinction we have been pointing out between *old* and *terrible in appearance* is the distinction between *restrictive* and *non-restrictive* modifiers, whether adjective, adverb, phrase, clause, or appositive.

Sometimes, even with no change whatsoever in the wording of his sentence, a writer may indicate the degree of relationship he has in mind: *They went on Tuesday to the horse market. They went, on Tuesday, to the horse market.* In the second sentence *on Tuesday* is far less important than in the first. A person speaking either of these sentences would spontaneously show which meaning he intended. Interruptions within the sentence are set off by a pair of commas.

Nonrestrictive modifiers that occur either before or after the basic sentence are set off by one comma:

● Sentence modifiers: *Of course, it was an unpardonable mistake. In the first place, you were within your rights. You may go, certainly. He was a fool, I thought. It was largely in the nature of an experiment, to be sure.*
● Verbals: *Turning the corner, I found myself on a busy street. He came toward me, grinning like a fool. For doing this, you will receive ten dollars. You will find this an aid, whether for writing or for speaking. To start the car, you must first turn the ignition key. You don't have to swear, to start a car. To tell you the truth, the man is a fool.*
● Nominative absolute: *The sun having set, I went home. They accomplished their purpose easily, the way having been prepared for them. I send you ten dollars now, the rest to come next week.*

There are other uses of the comma:

● Addresses and dates: *He went to Chicago, Illinois. The date was March 13, 1941.* A tendency noticeable at present is to omit the comma after the name of a state or country and after the number expressing the year: *On March 3, 1941 he went to Chicago, Illinois for a year.*

- Series: *We study algebra, chemistry, and history. The children bought yellow, white, and green balloons. He went to the drugstore, to the meat market, and to the bakery.*
- Coordinate adjectives: *He wore an old, tattered coat.* If the adjectives are not coordinate, no comma is used: *He lived in an old brick house.* The distinction in punctuation of coordinate and non-coordinate adjectives is passing out of use.
- Interjections and words of address: *Oh, I don't think so. No, you need not go. James, you must not go. Henry, why did you go? Where are you going, John?* More vehement exclamations and words of address may be followed by an exclamation mark: *Here! Listen to me. Idiot! What are you trying to do!*
- Appositives: Appositives which are not essential for the identification of the noun to which they are attached are set off by commas: *Our bookkeeper, Miss Jones, can tell you the story.* (The difference between such an appositive and a word of address can be learned only by hearing the sentence spoken or seeing it in its context. Is Miss Jones the bookkeeper or is she the person spoken to?)

Commas constitute perhaps half of all the marks of punctuation used in composition. Two other marks, however, are often used to indicate breaks in the flow of thought. One of these is the dash to convey the notion of a sudden break or of a repetition: *The day was hot—very hot. Won't you do this for me—like a good boy? The next day—Tuesday, perhaps—the Admiral visited Norwich.*

Parenthesis marks are used as their name indicates—to insert material within the sentence: *The next day (Tuesday) the Admiral visited Norwich. He meant (so he said) to remain there a week.*

COMPOUND SENTENCES

There is little to say about the punctuation of the compound sentence. The matter is one of joining two or more clauses together. There are two kinds of compound sentences—those in which a conjunction is expressed and those in which it is not. If no conjunction is present, a semicolon is ordinarily—but by no means universally—used: *They usually went to town by the valley road; in times of high water, they went by the hill road.* Even in a sentence with no conjunction, however, a comma is often used, as in Julius Caesar's famous line: *I came, I saw, I conquered.*

The use of a comma instead of a semi-colon in a compound sentence in which no conjunction is expressed leads to that bugaboo—worst of all sins in composition—a comma splice. Two clauses that have no connection with each other should not be joined by a comma; but they should not be joined by a semicolon either if they have no connection with each other. Two such clauses have no business being joined at all. Therefore the objection to the comma splice is merely an objection to a bad sentence. On the other hand, there are many sentences in which a comma is a far more effective means of giving unity and speed to a sentence than a semicolon could possibly be: *He always knew the right thing to say, he always knew the right thing to do.* Insofar as a comma splice substitutes for a period, it is bad; insofar as it substitutes for a semicolon, that is a matter of the writer's discretion. It is safe to predict that the comma in such constructions will increase rather than decrease in use.

The distinction between sentences which are compound in meaning and those which are compound in form but complex in meaning is not very sharp. The matter is of no great importance, except to point out that in such cases a comma is perhaps preferable to a semicolon: *The asparagus is good this year, we have had much rain.* There is no justification for insisting (as some persons do) that a conjunction be supplied between the clauses. (Compound sentences are older than coordinating conjunctions.) Nor is there justification for insisting on a semicolon. Nor is there justification for condemning such a sentence on the ground of its being a "comma splice."

Compound sentences in which a coordinating conjunction appears are of two kinds: those with a simple conjunction and those with a conjunctive adverb. The distinction in punctuation (which seemingly is of decreasing importance) is to the effect that simple conjunctions are preceded by a comma but that conjunctive adverbs are preceded by a semicolon and followed by a comma if they contain more than one syllable:. *I went to town, but Mary stayed home.* (As often as not no comma is used in such sentences.) *I am busy now; nevertheless, I can see you soon.*

Like many other "rules," those with reference to simple and adverbial conjunctions have little validity today, for many writers use a comma before *so* and other conjunctions of one syllable: *I hadn't any money, so I couldn't go to the show. I waited for you an hour, then I went home.* It is possible that the semicolon before conjunctions of more than one syllable will eventually disappear also.

COMPLEX SENTENCES

Complex sentences present no new problems in punctuation.
Noun clauses, being integral parts of the sentence unit, require no punctuation: *That the world is round is true. I know that he will come. He had no money was his reason for staying here.*
Noun clauses used as quotations need special punctuation: *He said, "I will not do it." "Will you go?" he asked. "If you do not hurry," I said, "you will be late." "Are you," he asked, "going with me?" Did he ask, "Are you going with me?"*
Adjective clauses follow the same principles as other adjective modifiers. If they are essential to the nouns they modify, they require no punctuation: *The house which stands on the corner was sold recently.* If, however, the clause is not essential, it is set off by a comma: *My father, whom I visited recently, is an old man.* Many writers make little or no distinction in the punctuation of restrictive and nonrestrictive clauses. The context almost always makes the matter clear, commas or no commas.

Adverb clauses are less frequently set off with commas than they formerly were. The old rule that an adverb clause must be set off with a comma if it precedes its main clause, and not set off if it follows the main clause, is a statement now more honored in the breach than in the observance. The matter is one of closeness of relationship rather than of position: *That is the truth as far as I understand the matter. That is the truth, as far as I understand the matter. If you love me you will grant my request. If you love me, you will grant my request.*

When an adverb clause is felt to be an interruption in the flow of the sentence, it is, like any other such element, set off with commas: *What he wanted, as I understand the matter, was to sell the place outright.* Similarly, any adverb clause which is a sentence modifier is set off by a comma, whether it comes before the main clause or after it: *If you ask me, the man is a fool. The man is a fool, if you ask me.*

Index

Action verbs, 10
Active voice, 97
Address, words of, 58-59
Adjective clauses, 76-78
Adjectives, 9, 32-34
    Comparison, 52-53
    Coordinate, 33
    Predicate, 23
Adverb clauses, 78-82
Adverbial complements, 17
Adverbial conjunctions, 69
Adverbial objectives, 17, 36
Adverbs, 20, 34-37
    Comparison, 53
    Ending in -*ly*, 34, 39
    Sentence modifiers, 36
Agreement, of subject and predicate, 44-47
Analytic languages, 19
Antecedents, 77
Appositional sentences, 23
Appositives, 57-60
    Interjections, 57-58
    Simple, 57
    Words of address, 58-59

Attribute predicates, 22-27
Auxiliaries, 24

Be as a verb, 23-24

Case, 47-50
    Nouns, 47-49
    Pronouns, 49-50
Clauses, 72-83
    Adjective, 76-78
    Nonrestrictive, 78
    Restrictive, 78
    Adverb, 78-82
    Noun, 72-75
    Verb, 82-83
Commands, word order, 55
Commas, 108-110
Comma splices, 69-70
Comparison, 52-53
    Adjectives, 52-53
    Adverbs, 53
Complementary verbs, 25
Complements, 16-22
    Adverbial, 17
    Dative (indirect), 98

Object, 17
  Retained, 98-99
Complete verbs, 15-16
Complex sentences, 72-83
Compound sentences, 67-70
Compounds, 29-32
  Adjective, 31
  Adverb, 31
  Elements, 63-64
  Noun, 29-30
  Verb, 31
Conjunctions, 68-69
  Adverbial, 69
  Coordinating, 69
  Simple, 69
  Subordinating, 80
Consequential participles, 102
Context, defined, 14

Dangling participles, 101
Dashes, 110
Dative (indirect) complements, 98
Determinatives, 59, 72, 77, 79
Discontinuous verbs, 21

Exclamation marks, 108

Genitives, 48-49, 86-89
  Independent, 48
  Objective, 87
  Subjective, 87
Gerunds, 85-89

Identification predicates, 22
Impersonal verbs, 61
Incomplete verbs, 16
Infinitives, 89-95
  Prepositional, 91
  Simple, 89

Split, 94
  With *for*, 94
  With subject accusative, 92-93
Inflection, defined, 43
Intensives, 36-37
Interjections, 8, 57-58
Internal punctuation, 108-113
  Commas, 108-110
  Dashes, 110
  Parentheses, 110
  Semicolons, 111-112
Irregular verbs, 51
It as subject, 60-62

Modal auxiliaries, 24
Mode, defined, 24
Modifiers, 32-37
  Adjective, 32-34
  Adverb, 34-37
  Sentence, 36, 40, 100

Nominative absolutes, 102
Nominative of address, 58-59
Nonrestrictive clauses, 78
Notional verbs, 22
Noun clauses, 72-75
Nouns, defined, 8
  Formation of plurals, 44-45
  Person, 46-47
  Predicate, 23
Number, singular and plural, 44-46
  Nouns, 44-45
  Pronouns, 45-46
  Verbs, 46

Object complements, 17
Object genitives, 87

Parentheses, 110
Participles, 95-103
    Consequential, 102
    Dangling, 101
    Defined, 95
    Nominative absolutes, 102
    Sentence modifiers, 100
Particles, 38
Passive voice, 96-97
Periods, 107
Person, 46-47
    Nouns, 46
    Pronouns, 47
    Verbs, 47
Predicates, 15-27
    Adjective, 23
    Attribute, 22-27
    Defined, 10-11
    Descriptive, 22
    Identification, 22
    Noun, 23
    Verb, 15-22
Prepositional infinitives, 91
Prepositional phrases, 38-41
    Origin, 39-40
    Sentence modifiers, 40
Prepositions, 38-39
    Ending a sentence, 41
Progressive verb forms, 99
Pronouns, 45, 49-50
    Formation of plurals, 45
    Personal dropped as sign of
      subordination, 76
    Relative, 77-78
Punctuation, rhetorical function
    of, 106-107

Question marks, 107
Questions, word order, 56-57

Restrictive clauses, 78
Retained complements, 98-99
Rule of agreement, 44-47

Semicolons, 111-112
Sentence appositives, 59-60
Sentence context, 14
Sentence equivalents, 12
Sentence modifiers, 36, 40, 100
Sentence order, 55-57
    Commands, 55
    Questions, 56-57
Sentences, 7-13
    Complete verbs, 15-16
    Incomplete verbs, 16
Simple conjunctions, 69
Simple infinitives, 89
Simple sentence patterns, 14-27
Split infinitives, 94
Subject, defined, 11
Subjective genitives, 87
Subject-verb agreement, 44-47
Subordinating conjunctions, 80
Synthetic languages, 19

Tense, 50-52
Terminal punctuation, 107-108
    Exclamation marks, 108
    Periods, 107
    Question marks, 107
There as subject, 62-63

Verbals, 85-103
    Gerunds, 85-89
    Infinitives, 89-95
    Participles, 95-103

Verb clauses, 82-83
Verb complements, 16-22

118 Index

Verbs, defined, 10
   Auxiliaries, 24
   Complementary, 25
   Complete, 15-16
   Discontinuous, 21
   Formation of past tense,
     50-51
   Perfect-tense forms, 99-100

Progressive forms, 99
Voice, 96-97
   Active, 97
   Passive, 96-97

Word order, 17-19
Words of address, 58-59